Printed in the United States of America

First Printing, 2018

ISBN 9781980977704

Disclaimers:
The stories in this book reflect the author's recollection of events. Some names, locations, and identifying characteristics have been changed to protect the privacy of those depicted. Dialogue has been re-created from memory.

This book is not intended as a substitute for the medical advice of physicians. The reader should regularly consult a physician in matters relating to his/her health and particularly with respect to any symptoms that may require diagnosis or medical attention.

Cover photo by Lisa Denning, Ocean Eyes Photography
About the Author photo in ocean by Jeff Leicher
About the Author photo on land by Selian Hebald

Praise for Claire Elisabeth's
Reconcile

"Claire Elisabeth weaves a magical tale from loss to redemption that is reminiscent of the book **Eat, Pray, Love**. *Everyone who has (or has had) a mother needs to experience the healing power of this touching book."*

~ **L.H.** – Consultant

"Claire writes for all of us. She shares her life story with candid honesty and lighthearted humor. We are right there with her, healing ourselves alongside her. Countless times I thought she was peeking into my own memory bank, as I remembered having the very same thoughts and feelings that she was describing.

As you read her story, you'll feel it and know it: this is your love story, too. You are breathing hope into your own journey of healing and wholeness, just by believing this: that you, too, can clear through whatever is in the way of loving and birthing your true self."

~ **A.P.** – Psychotherapist

"Reconcile *reads like a poem."*

~ **B.G.** – Intuitive Counselor

"I lost count of how many times this book made me cry. Not because the story hurt me, but because the achingly honest beauty of her words refused to stop opening my heart. Claire's story is intensely personal, but in her telling, she shows us the insides of the universal process of turning grief into love."

~ **E.T.** – Writer, Coach

Reconcile

A True Tale of Love, Loss, and the Power to Heal

Claire Elisabeth

For my mom
Thank you

Author's Note

October 12, 2017
Kealakekua Bay

As I sat at the water's edge, listening to the waves rhythmically crash upon the shore, like the heartbeat of Mother Earth, I looked out at the ocean, as I often do, searching for a feeling of peace.

Today I looked for an extra dose of comfort from the turquoise sea.

My mother died one year ago today.

Here.

In these waters.

It was at this shore that five strangers carried her to land, tried to revive her, and ultimately called the ambulance that drove her to that cold room, placed her on that sterile table, and draped a sheet over her lifeless body.

One year later, I came to this beach, not because of the anniversary, but because I come every day. I still swim the 2 miles across the bay and back. I still relax on the shore after each swim. And I still gaze out at the waters. Mostly just taking in the glorious view, but sometimes, I must admit, I still stare out at the ocean and ask, "Why?" "How?"

Today, as I longingly looked to the sea for answers, I felt something pull me to the Earth. It was as if, all of a sudden, I weighed 1000 pounds. Gravity had never pulled so strongly.

The same force that pulled me towards the Earth also tucked my chin and steered my gaze downward. I saw a colony of ants criss-crossing a fallen leaf, surveying the terrain. A large, iridescent wasp flew in, but despite being 100 times the size of the ants, didn't seem to cause any change in the surveying process, and he quickly moved on.

I felt a presence, and I asked aloud, "Is that you, Mom?"

The force pulling me to the Earth now called me inward, and it had a voice.

"Come back to now," it said. "Come back to now."

My attention crept back into my body. Back from across the ocean. Back from one year ago when I stood on this shore in disbelief as the police asked me what my mother was wearing and what her name was.

Was.

"What *was* your mom's name?" the policeman asked.

"IS!" I shouted in my mind. "Her name IS Betty."

He was trying to tell me that she was no longer with us. But I couldn't hear it. Not yet. Not until I saw her unmoving body on that table did I believe my mother was now forever in *past tense.*

Coming back to now was not an easy task. That day one year ago is seductive. Painful, yes. But also seductive, as it beckons me to visit it again and again.

As I returned to the beach, still looking down and in, I asked, "How can I honor you, Mom?"

I heard:

Write this book.
Be yourself.
Glow.
I'm here with you.
You will be taken care of.

So I did.

Here it is.

The book my Mama, Mother Earth, and the Hawaiian spinner dolphins called me to write.

May it heal you to read as much as it healed me to write.

1
My first time

The first time I broke the law, I was five years old.

I walked into the grocery store with my dad's girlfriend Anita, who lovingly calls herself my 'SortaMom.' She had told me that people were doing awful things to dolphins, and "we have to do something!"

So we did.

We sauntered in, a woman and child. Unassuming. Except that we had something up our sleeves.

Literally.

We had stickers up our sleeves.

I know stickers might not seem like weapons of mass destruction, but to a five year old, this was a big deal.

We found the aisle with the offending commodity — tuna cans — and we proceeded to put stickers on all the cans.

They read: *DO NOT buy this product. Dolphins get caught and die in fishing line used to catch tuna. This is NOT dolphin-safe tuna.*

I felt like a rebel, a thug, and a hero all at once.

I was scared someone was going to come and arrest us, but it was worth it. I mean, we were *saving dolphins.*

We did not get arrested that day.

In fact, I don't think we were noticed at all, except by a 3-year-old boy who walked by with a quizzical and curious look. He probably wondered what was so exciting about these particular cans. Maybe they had magic gummy bears in them or something. Or maybe he could look right through us and he *knew,* like kids *know,* that we were up to no good.

Either way, he didn't tell on us, and we got away with it.

I came away from that experience with two powerful beliefs:

> 1- Dolphins are pretty much the coolest thing in the universe, and they're worth risking my life (or at least my reputation) for.
> 2- Doing what my heart says is right is more important than following the rules.

Number one set the stage for a life-long love affair with cetaceans.

Number two got me in a lot of trouble over the years.

2

Fear

My mom was always driven by fear.

Anxious about this. Fretting over that. Gasping at sudden movements. "Oh Gawd"-ing when she listened to a friend relay an issue that, according to my mom, deserved some worrying.

I grew up disliking fear, and I diligently worked to banish it from my own repertoire of emotions. It seemed to make my mother's life miserable, and I wanted nothing to do with it.

Alas, eliminating an instinctual response to danger proved impossible, but that didn't stop me from trying.

My mother, on the other hand, praised the virtues of fear. "I'll just have to worry us through this," she'd say when a difficult situation presented itself. She often told me of the time she "worried me to health" when I was just a wee one in her belly.

When she was pregnant with me, she took a prescription drug her doctor had advised she take for a stubborn bout of bronchitis she couldn't seem to shake.

She didn't yet know she was pregnant. Her doctor didn't either. The drug was perfectly safe as long as you *weren't* pregnant.

Oops.

When she found out she was pregnant, she panicked. When the doctor found out, he suggested she consider an abortion.

She obviously didn't abort me. Instead, she chose her preferred tried-and-true method of surviving anything. "I worried us all through those nine months," she reassured me.

Um. Thanks. I think.

When I was born, I wouldn't breathe. My mother immediately began worrying me through that one too, but my father wasn't so facile at manifesting happy endings through fear. So he promptly fainted, crashing into a tray of cotton swabs and rubber gloves.

When he came to, he was white as a sheet, but lucid. And I was no longer blue. In fact, the doctor had proclaimed me a "healthy girl." In his expert opinion, I had not suffered any ill effects from either the bronchitis drug or the lack of oxygen.

"Ah," said my father. "We're in the clear. Let's call her Claire."

3
Mom

My parents divorced when I was three, and my mom didn't remarry until I had a child of my own, so growing up it was pretty much just the two of us. We did fine while I was little and I still considered my mom a 'knower' as I used to say, but once I was old enough to have fully formed thoughts about the important things in life—love, liberty, and what color my bedroom walls should be—we ran into trouble.

You see, my mom and I were not cut from the same cloth. The chasm between her worldview and mine was vast. And it wasn't just empty space that filled the canyon between us. There were banana peels, booby traps, and electric eels. Miscommunications. Misinterpretations. Old hurts making appearances at inopportune moments. Jagged edges of attempted apologies that scraped against bruised egos. If we were lucky, it was a delicate dance between us. If we weren't so lucky, it was a minefield.

The mudslinging usually began with something small. A little criticism. An unapproving look. A "Well, of course you're going to…"

No. I likely wasn't going to.

She wanted me to talk sweetly to the guests. I wanted to hide in my room and avoid the pain of putting on a fake smile and pretending to like people.

She wanted me to walk a certain way and talk a certain way and do my hair a certain way because, "Claire, you could be beautiful if only…" I wanted to wear ripped jeans and a baseball cap and not be known for what I looked like.

She wanted me to be a doctor. I wanted to be an artist.

She liked others to approve of her, and of me, and of her as a mother by virtue of my behavior. I liked to speak my mind. Loudly.

And then there was the small stuff:

She loved to plan. I loved to not worry about Saturday's dinner on Wednesday.

She loved to dress up. I loved to spend all week in the same pajamas.

She loved to go out on the town. I loved to stay home and pet the cat.

And on and on it went.

We never lost our love for one another, but we didn't always *like* each other.

But it wasn't always a struggle either.

Amidst the launchings of "Don't defy me" and "I want to rip your lungs out," my mom would also lob these my way:

Claire-Dee-Boo, you're magical.
I'm so lucky to be your mom.
I love you bigger than the world.

And it was real. All of it was real. Her painful breakdowns over my insubordination were real. My hatred of her worldview was real. And our unending love for each other was real.

Mom and I had deep love and massive incompatibility rolled into one giant food fight of a relationship.

4
Good Girl

Thirteen years after my first experience as a dolphin-saving heathen in the tuna aisle at Safeway, I moved to the Left Coast, as my father called it, to attend the University of California, Berkeley. The mecca of tie dye, LSD, political upheaval, and outrageous thinkers—it was like 'Berkeley' and 'rebel' were synonymous. I was going to fit right in.

Except that something came over me during my transition out of the nest and into the wild. Maybe I thought it was time to 'grow up.' Or maybe the 'should' voice had finally worn me down. In any case, I turned off my rebel and I turned on my 'good girl.'

I was pre-med. Organic chemistry, calculus, physics, anatomy. I was also double majoring in Spanish. And I was getting straight A's.

I was also racing in triathlons, and was president of the triathlon club.

I was smart, fit, cute, had my life all planned out, and now I was even nice.

I was the girl everyone loved to hate.

But it didn't last.

I mean, the hatred lasted.

But the good life didn't.

It was a Thursday. I went out for my normal 10 mile run, and about 6 miles in I began to have some pretty intense ankle pain. But I was on the fire trail above campus, and all I could do was keep running until I got home.

Well, truth be told, I could have taken the bus, but I had too much pride and was in too much denial for that.

So I ran until I couldn't run anymore. Then I walked. Then I hobbled. Once I got in the door, I crawled.

For weeks all I did was crawl from my bedroom, to the bathroom, to the kitchen, and back to my bedroom.

After a month or so, I managed to get myself hobbling around enough to drive myself to doctors of all kinds. Western, Eastern, traditional, non-traditional, down-to-Earth, woo-woo... Nothing helped. In fact, everything made it worse.

The powers that be told me pain can only be managed. Take 10 Advil each day for the rest of your life. Stop running. Lower your expectations. Let go of your dreams.

5
Let Go of Your Dreams

"Let go of your dreams."

Those words pummeled me like ice-cube sized hailstones — the ones that come when the sky is yellow, right before the big tornado.

Despite the hailstorm in my mind (or maybe because of it) I did get myself walking again. I was fueled by my overactive willpower, hatred for the authorities, and a determination to prove them wrong.

Mind you, I didn't walk fast. No, it was more like I gingerly crept along the sidewalks and hallways, every step calculated, placing just as much weight on my heels, ankles, and toes as I could bear. A stumble could be devastating. A twisted ankle would set me back months.

So I crept to campus. A walk that used to take 10 minutes now took an hour. But I got there.

I even dared to go on a field trip with my plant biology class to the redwood forests. We piled on the bus like 2nd graders and bounced along for 2 hours to our destination. Plant biology wasn't my favorite class by a long shot, but I must admit it was pretty cool to be surrounded by 200-year-old trees, to smell the damp forest floor, and to be greeted by the sun-shiny oxalis pes-caprae flowers, beaming their bright yellow petals at us like children smiling at the sky.

We collected samples for our ever-growing collection of living flashcards, and took notes on the tour from the park ranger. That is, until my body said, 'no more.'

It wasn't my feet or ankles this time. They were doing amazingly well, keeping me upright and mobile for the excursion. This time it was my arm. I was dutifully taking notes on the deathly boring lecture, and my right arm went completely limp. Not numb, but lifeless. My pen dropped to the ground and I could no longer move my fingers or my wrist. It was as if someone opened up the control panel in my brain and just flipped the 'right arm' switch to the OFF position.

First there was a level of disbelief, and then came resignation.

"Let go of your dreams" played on repeat.

And once again, the doctors were stumped. Perhaps it was nerve damage. Or repetitive stress syndrome. Carpal tunnel was in vogue at the time, and several doctors suggested I get carpal tunnel surgery, even though they weren't sure if that was the problem.

No thanks.

As best I could, I took matters into my own hands again. At least the one that was working.

I would hobble to class and take notes with my left hand. It took up a whole page to write one sentence, and my notebook looked like it had been hijacked by a 2-year-old or a stroke victim. Only I could tell the lines sprawled across the page were even words.

6
Drastic Measures

As they say, drastic times call for drastic measures.

I had tried the doctors, the tests, and the prescription drugs.

I had tried acupuncture, yoga, and physical therapy.

I had tried Ecstasy in hopes of finding a single moment of…well…ecstasy, but that led to a gran mal seizure that by all medical accounts should have left me with serious brain damage.

I had even tried prayer, although I don't think I was very nice. It was more like a silent tirade against the universe.

Ok, maybe I didn't try prayer.

But I did decide that it was time to go off-roading with my therapy.

As I was walking to the post office in downtown Berkeley, I saw an old, spooky building that looked like it came right out of the scene in Ghostbusters where the Zuul cat breaks out of its concrete form on its way to demonically possess Sigourney Weaver.

There was a sign in the front window that said, "Meditation 1 starts Wednesday."

This was just the off-roading I needed — meditation taught by Zuul cats.

So I went inside.

I was greeted by a woman with blond hair that reached past her butt. She wore jeans, cowboy boots, and leg warmers. Don't ask me how that combination was possible. She did it. She smiled, and asked me to have a seat on what looked like a church pew.

"Would you like a healing?"

Not what I expected from a meditation teacher, but *Hell Yes* I want a healing!

She rubbed her hands together, looked off to the upper left corner of the room as if summoning some unseen force, and then proceeded to wave her hands all around me, pausing at times to grab something invisible and flick it off to the side, laughing as she did it.

She put her hands above my head a few times and appeared to be pulling something down from above my 'space' as she called it.

"You're very far away from your body," she said. "Did you have a recent trauma?"

"Well," I said, "I just got out of the hospital after having a drug-induced gran mal seizure."

She laughed.

Then yawned.

"Cool," she said.

No. I thought. Not cool. But whatever she was doing felt good, so I resisted the urge to smack her.

Then she did something that forever changed my view of what is real.

She hovered her hands above my forearms and swept the air towards my fingertips, then flicked her hands again, like she was clearing cobwebs off of my arms and shaking them to the floor.

For the first time since that moment in biology class when my arm went dead, I had no pain in my wrists.

"What did you just do?"

"Oh I just cleared some brown energy from your creative channels."

Uh. Ok. Thanks.

Whatever creative channels were, clearing them made my pain go away.

I was in.

I didn't understand it, and on many levels I didn't believe it, but I knew I needed to learn whatever this woman knew.

So I spent the better part of the next three years in that old, dilapidated building. Mostly with my eyes closed, thank goodness.

I waved my arms around hundreds of other people, laughing, yawning, and flicking brown energy out of their space.

I also learned to do energy readings (less hand waving, more yawning) and to clear my own space of foreign (not always brown) energy.

It was clearing one's own space, or 'running energy' as they called it, that they advertised as meditation. Not your run-of-the-mill 'think of nothing' meditation, but hey, it was Berkeley and it was helping.

I don't think I ever fully believed in what I was doing — reading past lives, clearing people's chakras, peering into the future…but it didn't matter.

I would sit for hours each day, watching colors and images in my mind's eye, and it made me feel better.

7

Na'au

In Hawaiian culture, and in the Hawaiian shamanic practice of Huna[1], the most revered teachers and elders are not the ones with the most knowledge, or even with the highest IQs. Rather, the yardstick by which respect and honor is given is how connected you are to your instincts. The Hawaiians believe the seat of intuition lies in the belly, near the location Traditional Chinese Medicine calls the *dantien*. In Hawaiian, it is called your *na'au*.

Those who are most connected to their na'au are the masters. The leaders. And the shamans—those who speak freely with the ancestors, the ocean, and who walk in both the physical and spiritual worlds.

Your na'au is so important, say the shamans, because it is the gateway to your Higher Self. Your Higher Self is all-knowing—it's connected to your past, your future, Spirit, Earth, and everything in between. It knows all the things you'd ever want a crystal ball to show you, but it won't share its knowledge with your monkey mind. No, your Higher Self speaks only to your na'au, so to be

---

[1] All information in this book regarding Huna comes from teachings I received from the Bray family lineage of this Hawaiian art.

connected to the answers as the shamans are, you need to make friends with your gut.

I had a long way to go, as my most profound connection with my gut was chronic stomach aches.

8
Ecstasy

Confession: I wasn't just trying to escape my physical pain when I took Ecstasy. I was trying to fit in. Trying to be liked. Trying to be the cool kid I thought I should be, but wasn't.

For as long as I could remember, I always had two voices in my head. The voice of who I wanted to be, and the voice of who I thought I should be. I hadn't even met the voice of who I really was.

The voices of 'who I want to be' and 'who I should be' did not get along. They'd put on their brass knuckles and duke it out in my mind, 2 a.m. being their favorite time to get in the ring. I'd be trying to get a moment of shut-eye and there they were, kicking and throwing sucker punches at each other.

It's a miracle I ever slept through the night. Or made a decision.

I wouldn't have made the ranks of shaman in any traditional society. I probably wouldn't have even been allowed to say "shaman" had I been born into a community that had one.

And when I took that little white pill and put it in my mouth, I certainly wasn't listening to sage advice from Spirit. Rather, I was listening to a voice that said, "He'll finally accept you if you do this."

'He' was my boyfriend, and he was smart, charming, outgoing... We had been together for 5 years and I was sure he was 'the one.' I'm not sure what he thought of me, but I know the way I felt when I was around him.

Amazing. And lousy.

Beautiful. But not stylish or sexy enough.

Wicked smart. But not putting my intelligence to work for anything useful.

Fun. But not outgoing enough.

You see, I was a nerd. I wasn't exactly shy, but I didn't like parties (still don't.)

I didn't like to go out with his friends, and it was a consistent point of contention.

One Valentine's Day, I gave in.

I did something totally out of character, that I didn't want to do, because I thought my boyfriend would love me more if I did it.

I thought maybe he would finally accept me, and I could relax and be happy.

Instead, I had a seizure, nearly bit my tongue off, dislocated my shoulder, went into a coma, and defied all odds to even wake up.

Not really a good trade for the slim chance that someone would like me more.

I lost a piece of myself with the choice I made that night.

It was as if I banished a fragment of my soul the moment I took that little white pill out of its tiny baggie.

And my deal with the devil didn't even work. I was still the uncool kid. Only now I was the uncool kid who almost died trying to be cool.

9
Dolphins

I spent obscene amounts of time in the Zuul cats meditation castle, but I didn't consider myself a meditator, or an energy healer, or, God forbid, a clairvoyant reader, even though those were all words that got thrown around nearly as much as 'brown energy' and 'space.'

I guess you could call me a *closet* energyworker.

Who else spends 15 hours a week intently practicing a skill and then pretends to have nothing to do with it?

Maybe those voices in my head were starting to do permanent damage.

But there was one thing I was certain of.

There was a poster on the wall outside of my favorite teacher's office and it had pictures of dolphins on it. Pictures that she had taken. In the water. With wild spinner dolphins.

Carmen took several 'podners,' as she called them, to the Big Island of Hawaii each year for a meditation retreat that involved swimming with wild dolphins. Sometimes she captured a blurry, blissful moment on film, and some of those moments ended up on the wall outside of her office.

I walked by that poster a thousand times, and each time I would pause and stare at the grainy underwater photos of blurred dolphins, imagining what it might be like to be there. I probably would have continued this ritual for another thousand days, but something inside me finally spoke up.

It told me that I had to stop walking right by the one thing I knew I must do. I had to stop swooning and foaming at the mouth over out-of-focus photos. I had to get myself into those waters.

My gut had finally found a functioning connection to the parts of me that I actually paid attention to, and it was sending me a clear message — dolphins.

One word. Two syllables. I got the memo.

I paid for the trip with money I didn't have, and I didn't care. I knew, possibly for the first time in my life, that *all of me* wanted to do something. I had to go.

10
Hawaii

The moment I stepped off the plane, I began to sweat.
You see, the Kona airport is entirely outside. And there's
no air-conditioned corridor. No corridor at all, actually.
You get up from your seat, walk to the front (or the back)
of the airplane, and down a set of stairs on to the tarmac.
The airport employees are always nice and have plenty
of aloha, but that doesn't change the fact that it's about
400 degrees warmer here than wherever you came from.

So I began to sweat. And not just that 'glow' that some
people get that looks cheerful and healthy. Beads were
forming on my upper lip and in my armpits, like you'd
expect from a normal sweat-er. But I was going for the
gold medal here—sweat was dripping down my back,
pooling in my waistband. It was dripping down my legs,
as if I were peeing the slightest trickle of pee for the
better part of an hour. I think my hair was even
sweating.

We drove past barren fields of lava rock and a very small
industrial area before turning down Palani Street and
arriving at the center of town—a few short blocks
packed with every Hawaiian tourist attraction you could
think of. There were swim shops, t-shirt shops, jewelry
shops, coffee shops, parrots that would sit on your

shoulder and say "hang loose" while you snapped a photo, storefronts offering zip-line rides, manta ray night dives, and of course, dolphin adventures. You could get fresh fish tacos, a papaya-guava-pineapple smoothie, buy a titanium wedding ring, and rent a kayak all on the same block.

But we were just passing through.

The ocean was calling.

After heaping my luggage on the pull-out couch that would be my bed for the next week, and taking off every bit of sweat drenched clothing I was wearing, I put on one of the five (yes five) swimming suits I had brought, and headed for Turtle Bay.

We were too late for the dolphins today, Carmen told us, but we could practice using our snorkel gear while hanging out with sea turtles. That worked for me.

I had never used a snorkel before, and I was using borrowed fins that looked like they were from medieval Europe compared to everyone else's fancy gear. But when we all got in the water, I was the one that 'went native' as Carmen said. It was as if my ill-fitting snorkel and medieval fins became part of me, and I was as happy as a humuhumunukunukuapua'a (the Hawaiian state fish) in the water.

11
Kealakekua Bay

Carmen said that there were three main bays where the dolphins frequent[2]. They're all within a 30-minute drive from each other, so this morning our plan was to start at the closest bay and work our way South.

Kealakekua Bay was our first stop. It is 4 miles down a narrow, winding street called Napoopoo Road. The Hawaiian language pronounces each vowel separately, so the name isn't as funny aloud as it is in print, but none of us knew that, so we all began to giggle like four-year-olds as we drove down the majestic winding road. Potty humor dies hard, even in paradise.

We arrived at the bottom of the road and were greeted by an elderly Hawaiian lady sitting in a dilapidated lawn chair. She grinned a gorgeous toothless grin, made an undulating up-and-down motion with her left hand, and said, "They're here."

We turned into the parking lot and frantically grabbed our excessive amount of gear. We were tourists after all, trying desperately to have all the trappings of the

---

[2] The spinner dolphins are protected by both state and federal law. If you choose to be near them in the water, please follow the guidelines in Appendix 4.

islanders in hopes of being mistaken for locals. So, of course, we all stood out like sore thumbs.

The Big Island has an interesting definition of 'beach.' Anywhere water meets land is considered a beach, even if, like here, it's really just a huge pile of tumbled lava rocks. But we didn't care. If this is how the locals meet the gods of the ocean, we were up for the task.

"Don't put your fins on while you're on the beach," said Carmen. "Carry them into the water like this." She effortlessly slipped into the water, arranged her fins, and began swimming towards the leaping and spinning pod of dolphins.

I dove in after her, and although all I could see in every direction was BLUE—sky blue, azure, turquoise, cerulean—I could hear the most amazing sounds. Squeaks, clicks, sustained high-pitched calls, all swimming through the water to my ears. These dolphin songs seemed to touch me, massage my cells, rearrange my molecules.

The dolphins actually seemed interested in me. They were curious, kind, even vulnerable. They swam right up to me, coming within inches of me, trusting me to keep my hands to myself, as they circled around me, dove beneath me, and jumped in graceful arcs above me.

But it was more than their physical closeness that struck me. Something happened when they looked me in the eye and swam so close to me.

It was if they could see a part of me that I never knew existed. A piece of me that was unencumbered with thoughts of being less-than, incomplete, or not-yet something or someone I thought I should be.

All of the not-enoughness that I'd carried on my shoulders and in my heart for decades...it vanished in their presence.

I was left with whoever it was that had been sleeping underneath all the anxiety and pain. "Is this *me*?" I wondered.

All of this transcendence had me forget about my body for a while, but I soon slammed back into present time when my ankles began to sear in pain.

Was I going to have to go back to shore?

As soon as I had that thought, a large dolphin came over to me and bobbed his head as if to say, "wassup?" (Or as the islanders say, "howzit?")

I'd like to say I began speaking fluently in dolphin squeaks and clicks, but the truth is, I just floated there like a very large and damaged piece of seaweed.

The dolphin swam directly beneath me, and blew a ring of bubbles above his head.

Immediately, the intercom in my mind came on and said, "Swim through the bubbles." I had no idea where that voice came from, but I figured I had nothing to lose, so I obeyed.

I swam down through the bubbles, and as I did, I heard "bup bup bup" — dolphin sonar.

And when I emerged on the surface of the water again, my pain had completely disappeared.

The pain that began on mile 6 during my run in the Berkeley hills. The pain that no doctor or healer seemed to have the ability to cure. The pain that had defined much of my life for the past three years. It disappeared.

12
Friendship for No Advantage

The Greek historian Plutarch is quoted as saying, "To the dolphin alone, beyond all other, nature has granted what the best philosophers seek: Friendship for no advantage."

Friendship for no advantage…Was that what caused the disappearance of my pain? Had my cells rearranged themselves within this field of total acceptance?

Whatever magic these dolphins had, it captivated me. I was the first one in the water each day, and the last one out, spending hours swimming alongside my new finned friends, attempting to soak up as much of their wisdom as I possibly could in the short time I was on the island.

I learned to relax amid my excitement, and to hold my breath long enough to take short dives down with the pod. I learned how to tell when the dolphins were sleeping, and when they wanted to interact. I learned how to play the leaf game with them — their delightful game of underwater tag. And I learned how to keep my body and mind still enough that the dolphins would come within centimeters of me, even when they were snoozing.

My physical pain never did return. Nor did my feelings of not-enoughness. I had been permanently and fundamentally altered by my contact with the spinners. And although I doubt I had such a profound effect on them, they did seem to take to me.

Babies would swim right up to me, catch my eye, and then leap into the air, like kids shouting, "Look Ma, no hands!" as they career down the hill on their bicycles. Older dolphins would circle me and swim by my side for what felt like hours.

On the last day of my inaugural visit to the Kona coast, I woke up at half past zero so I could get a swim in before the plane ride back to the mainland. A few others from the group went with me. We got in the water at 6 a.m. for our farewell swim, and there was a pod of about 60 dolphins in the bay to greet us. We danced and squeaked with our aquatic friends for just under an hour. Since I had a watch, it was my job to corral everyone, so at 6:45 I herded our human pod towards the shore.

After everyone else had climbed up the rocky shore, I looked back across the bay, at the fins and tails of my new friends as they surfaced to breathe, and I seriously considered not going home.

A young dolphin, perhaps sensing my hesitation to do what I must do, came up to my left side and looked me in the eye. I felt that deep sense of being seen, and this time it felt like he had just x-rayed my entire life. Like he knew all I'd been through, all I would go through in the future, and he, like a wise grandfather, was helping me to take that one next step that I was resisting. That one next step that would lead to all the other steps he knew I needed to take.

He kept my gaze as he escorted me to shore.

Back to my world.

Away from his.

For now.

*I got my very own blurry underwater photo on that trip.
Here I am waving at my new friends.
~photo by Carmen Figueras*

13
Pono

In Hawaiian, the word 'pono' means 'right,' but 'pono' isn't the opposite of 'wrong.' Rather, pono means to be right with one's self. To be aligned, undivided, fully in-tune and at peace with who you really are. To not be at war with yourself.

When you're pono, your physical life is in line with your heart, your values, and with the Great Spirit by whatever name you call her. You receive communication from your Higher Self in dreams, gut feelings, and instincts. And because your Higher Self is connected to All-That-Is, you are in-tune with the physical and non-physical worlds, like the shamans.

In my mind, this was the message from, and the magic of, the dolphins. They seemed to have this ability to catalyze a self-to-self connection, and to induce 'friendship for no advantage' with oneself.

When the not-enoughness fell away from my shoulders, and I felt like who I was might be okay, it was as if the lines of communication between the voices in my head, my heart, and my gut all opened up. Everyone began listening instead of fighting. Cordial lines formed in my psyche and mobs dissipated. My entire being relaxed, and in so doing, the wisdom of my cells, my DNA, and, the Hawaiians would add, my ancestors, all aligned and bowed their heads in service of my purpose.

Pono.

14
Nai'a Healing

'Nai'a' is the Hawaiian word for 'dolphin.' It also means 'to flow' and is used to describe free-spirited people who follow their hearts. To me, 'nai'a' had achieved regal status. I pretty much equated it with 'the answer to the Universe.'

I came back to the mainland energized with purpose, and, to the chagrin of my friends and family, carrying a passionate soapbox that I would rattle off at any given moment, to any willing (and many unwilling) listeners. I used to joke that I needed a portable step stool that I could take with me wherever I went, so I could properly proselytize my new belief that anything that ails you can be cured by being true to yourself. By becoming pono.

The dolphins had catalyzed this healing for me, and I was their spokesperson, their ambassador, bringing the dolphin wisdom to land. My singular focus was to help others in the way the spinners had helped me. To have *conversations* that were curative in the same way my swims had been.

So I created a healing modality, and I wouldn't shut up about it.

Although I bored throngs of people to pieces, most notably my family, with my never-ending stream of impromptu lectures, I did, in fact, have a point.

Nai'a Healing[3], as I coined it, worked.

I spent years working with people in my little home office, doing my best to bring what the shamans would call the 'dolphin medicine' into the room. We weren't swimming. I didn't have sonar. All I had was the memory of how it felt to be with the spinners, the conviction that healing comes from within, and my one magical healing gift — words.

I watched people recover from back pain, hip pain, and heart pain. I saw people overcome diagnoses of autism and irritable bowel disease. I witnessed others on the verge of divorce, and even suicide, turn their lives around. All of this happened when those who were suffering finally connected to that piece of themselves that the dolphins had awoken in me. That piece that looks candidly and piercingly at who you really are and says, "Yup, that's me. I'm a bundle of unique talents, glaring inabilities, and annoying habits. I embrace *all* of me."

---

[3] Nai'a Healing is based on the principle that being true to yourself is curative. To get a glimpse of what this process looks like, you can take the Nai'a Healing Questionnaire in Appendix 1.

I received a 'thank you' card from one of my clients that read, "You make me feel like I'm OK. Like whoever I am is who I'm supposed to be."

Yes.

That was my life for over a decade. I was the land dolphin. The one who would look you in the eye and see into your soul. The one who would create a *temenos* in the room — a sacred circle where you can be yourself without fear. I witnessed what felt like miracles, day in and day out.

And yet, while I spent my days guiding clients of all shapes and sizes to health and happiness, my own life began to silently and invisibly fall apart — finances, friendships, I didn't even have satisfying bowel movements anymore.

As the enlightened healer that I was, I took the opportunity to blame everything and everyone I could think of. It was my mom's fault. My dad's fault. My husband's fault. It was society. Motherhood. The fact that I didn't go to medical school like I was supposed to.

Of course, it was nobody's fault. I just needed a dose of my own medicine.

I knew that the only times I felt free and fully in-tune with myself were the times I spent on the island. In the ocean.

So I returned.

15
Home

Leaves in hand, I took three rapid breaths…and held the last one.

I plunged my head into the water and began to undulate my entire body, aiming my focus about 20 feet down.

When I reached my destination, I began placing the leaves in line, so they floated in the turquoise sea.

I emerged on the surface of the water and waited…

Here they came.

Six majestic spinner dolphins, ready to play.

They each took a leaf. One with his beak, another with her tail, and the rest with their fins. We danced around each other for what seemed like hours, passing the leaves back and forth among the pod.

They had let me in.

For a brief moment, I was an honorary dolphin.

We danced. We spun. We twirled. We squeaked. Yes, I squeaked too. I probably said something horribly offensive, but they didn't shun me for it.

Then they began to make swirling toroidal bubbles, and toss them to each other in the most magical game of catch I had ever seen. It looked as if the bubbles were alive—like they were little jellyfish leaping from one dolphin to the next.

One of the dolphins tossed me a jelly-bubble, not realizing that as a clumsy human, the moment I touched it, it would pop.

I wanted to abandon my humanness and live among these beautiful creatures forever.

As I emerged from the water, crawling on all fours up the rocky shore, I felt a magnetic pull to the Earth. It was as if someone turned the gravity dial up to 11. Sure, I had wobbly sea-legs, but this was more than that.

I couldn't resist the pull, so I finally gave in and lay down on a flat-ish mound of tumbled lava rocks.

"Home," I heard in my head, as I sank into the rocks and received the hug the island was offering me.

Legend says that we humans are here on Earth because dolphins brought us from the stars in celestial canoes. The dolphins are still here, by choice, as our guides and guardians.

Perhaps the dolphins were continuing their stewardship of me that day, guiding me home to the island.

16
The Move

I had no idea how I'd make the move, but I told a woman who I'd recently befriended at the beach that I was having thoughts of making the Big Island my permanent residence.

"A lot of people come here and they burn out," she said. "The island can eat you up and spit you out. The key is to remember you're not in charge. Surrender to the island."

Surrender wasn't my greatest talent. It wasn't even on a list of things I might consider doing. Ever.

In fact, I'm not sure I could properly define 'surrender,' which is probably why the next several months felt like I had been stuffed into a washing machine that was permanently set to 'agitate.'

Of course, all of the pain was self-inflicted.

I was the one who called the realtor in Hawaii. I was the one who, after seeing a house on my favorite 'potty humor in paradise' street — Napoopoo — decided to jump on a plane *the next day* to check it out. I was the one who decided to purchase the house without anyone else having seen it, and without the funds to complete the transaction.

It was *all me.*

But we did it. We. My husband, our son, our cat, my dad, and me. We jumped ship. Said sayonara to society. We boxed up everything we could fit in an 8 x 10 x 20 foot container, and headed out across the Pacific. When we all got on the plane in July 2016, I was the only one who'd even seen the house. The others gave me trust and loyalty beyond anything I could have earned, following me across the ocean like soldiers following a general into battle.

And somehow, we landed, quite smoothly, in the Hawaiian countryside.

Two short months after the day I introduced my father to his new home, he turned to me and said the most spiritual thing he'd ever said — "It's as if it was meant to be...if you believe in that kind of thing."

17
Two Eggs No People

Hawaii had guided us in for a soft landing, but it didn't give us a free pass.

We faced off against mosquitoes, cockroaches, torrential rain and wind storms, 5 power outages in 5 weeks, a hurricane scare, and the coqui frogs that sing their mating song so loudly through the night that you need to hit yourself over the head with a hammer to get any sleep.

These new Hawaiian battles were unnerving, but we managed to come out victorious on all accounts. Everyone was feeling pretty smug. Everyone but me, that is. I was terrified.

We were about to have guests.

And guests are terrifying.

You see, I'm what I call an extreme introvert.

Silence is my favorite place. It's where I feel most at home. Most relaxed. And most alive. It's also where I meet most of my best ideas. When it's quiet, I can hear them scuttling by, and sometimes I can entice them to come and play.

In silence, I'm tapped into the Thinkers' Zone. I imagine this is like the Athletes' Zone, where baseballs become the size of dinner plates and you just can't miss your target.

For me, it's thoughts that slow down and become catchable. Once one is in my hands, I can hold it up at any angle. Peer inside. Turn it upside down and shake it to see what's been lurking inside. I can even dismantle it, piece by piece, examining how each piece adheres to every other piece, or where there might be a hole, a gap that's ripe for a new creative burst. Silence is my happy place. My nirvana. My video arcade. My road trip. My party bus.

An actual party bus is more like being repeatedly poked in the eye with a stick.

Even gatherings — collections of my most adored friends chatting and laughing — inflict pain on my high-maintenance psyche.

So whenever possible, and at nearly any cost, I avoid groups of people.

And when I cannot avoid a celebration, it often takes me hours to recover.

Like one Sunday morning in late December a few years back, when our little family had a tiny early Christmas bash. My husband Soma was going to be out of town for the actual holiday, so we were opening presents early. We had a 3-inch tree that our son Felix had made out of felt, and there were a handful of presents, mostly for Felix, arranged around the tree.

With a proper amount of gift-opening excitement, Felix revelled in his new items, while also playing Santa and passing out the other presents to the rest of us.

The whole thing took about 15 minutes and I thought it was going to kill me. The moment he started playing with the walkie-talkies, and I heard that fuzzy screech sound as one receiver tried to connect with the other, I looked at my husband and said, "I've *got* to get out of here."

"Would you like some breakfast?" he called to me as I snuck down to the sanctuary that is my home office.

"Yes, please," I said. "Two eggs, no people."

18
The Guest

Truth be told, we weren't having guests.

We were having *a guest.*

A most wonderful and frightening guest.

My mom.

I had pleaded with her to give us four months to settle in and catch our breath, but she couldn't wait, so she was coming to visit after two. I wasn't ready. But, to be fair, I never was.

I told myself maybe this time would be different. Maybe I shouldn't feel so scared. After all, just before the move, Mom and I had a real moment of connection.

She and her husband Rick came to visit me in June. Well, what they really did was come to be saintly grandparents. Our house was on the market, and Soma and I were leaving town for a trip we had planned before I decided to take a spur-of-the-moment airplane ride across the Pacific and buy a house in Hawaii.

Mom and Rick were coming to be with Felix. That's what they signed up for, anyway. What they actually did was take care of Felix, keep the house absolutely spotless — sweep up after anyone took a step, wipe down the counters after anyone touched them, and basically clean every surface after it had been breathed on, in addition to manicuring the garden and maniacally hovering over the raised beds, waiting for a weed to have the audacity to sprout — plus they coordinated with realtors coming through with prospective buyers. We lived that way for a month, and it's a miracle nobody got seriously hurt. My mom and Rick endured it for seven days.

Soma and I came back from our trip and I was a wreck. I was terrified of what I was about to do. What I was leaving. The huge choice I had made for my family.

My mom and I took a walk around the neighborhood I was about to leave, and Mom listened. We often fought tooth and nail about things I now find irrelevant — manners, who was visiting whom for Christmas, whether 9 a.m. was too early to start talking about dinner — but when either one of us was in dire straights, we knew the other one would listen.

This was one of those times for me. Later, I would learn that it was one of those times for her too, but she was being Mommy here, and listening to her little girl panic.

And panic I did.

She offered to do a coaching technique with me that she had done several years previous — a visualization where you go 20 years into the future and chat with your future self.

The last time she did that with me, I was pregnant with my son. Very pregnant. It was one of those days where I ate breakfast, went to yoga, and then slept the rest of the day. I was living in the California house we were currently selling, and I was working as a healer. Well, I was mostly working as a napping, eating, baby-creator, but I did keep a few clients.

My mom and I had a great time chatting with my future self. I saw myself teaching people about love, which was in line with my current profession as a healer. But in the visualization I wasn't a healer. I was a writer. And I lived by the ocean. So close, in fact, that the ocean breeze was flowing through my future self's hair as I answered my 30-year-old self's questions.

So in my pre-Hawaii-move terror, my mom offered to do this same visualization with me again once she returned to Denver and she had all her notes. If my last future-self visualization had predicted a career change and a massive relocation, maybe this one would show me a future that would calm me down.

It did.

I saw myself in the newly purchased Hawaii house, which meant I was predicting I'd be there for at least 20 years.

I was exceedingly relaxed, like only an islander can be, in a flowing sarong-type jumper, and I kept saying, "Oh, Honey. Oh, Honey," to my younger self, as if to say, "Relax, everything will be okay."

But then the strangest thing happened. Not in my visualization, but on the phone with my mom.

She said, "I need to be done. I've given all I can give and I need to get something back."

I was in an altered state at this point in the call. Unaware of how much time had passed or what was going on in the 'real' world, I was completely focused on the movies that were playing in my mind.

I felt like someone had just hit me over the head with a frying pan, like they do in the cartoons.

Stars and birds were spinning above my head.

"Uh. Ok. What do you need, Mom?"

"I feel like I've been giving and giving and I'm not getting anything back."

"I'm so sorry. What do you need?"

"Do you realize that I've been grieving the loss of you for the last few months, since you told me you're moving?"

"Um. No. I had no idea. Why are you grieving? The phone knows no distance. And I'm following my dream. I'll be where I'm supposed to be. I feel like we're going to be closer when I move."

"I hope so. But I want you to know that I've been in a state of grief for the last few months. I've been holding it in around you, but I can't keep going like this. I can't keep giving and not getting anything back."

"Ok. So what do you need?"

"I think I need to tell you the things that have been bothering me. I feel like I'm always the last to know. I feel shut out. I feel like you don't let me in. You keep big life changes from me."

She was right. I did keep things from her. Especially big things. Over the years, I'd come to realize that my mom's judgments of me primarily stemmed from her judgments of *herself*. But that didn't change the fact that, when hurtled in my direction, they hurt.

As I listened to the pain in her voice, I could hear it was real. She wasn't making things up or trying to manipulate me.

And yet, several comments from the past began to replay in my head, and I remembered *why* I kept things from her...

You look like you don't have a mother.

You walk like a construction worker.

Why do you care if it's the weekend? You don't have any friends.

Do you realize how this reflects on ME?

Claire, your wedding isn't about you... it's about me.

And our endless conversations about my parenting approach...

Mom: *I worry you're not teaching Felix the right way to act in social situations.*
Me: *I'm teaching him to be himself.*
Mom: *That's not the point.*

I once had a conversation with a man named Barry who had, at one point, had a close friendship with my mom.

"Capitulation," he said. "I felt like being friends with your mother required capitulation. I had to choose between being friends with her and being friends with myself. I ultimately chose myself, but it wasn't easy. She had this way of making me second-guess all my instincts."

So, she was right. I shut her out. I didn't trust my most vulnerable thoughts to my own mother, because I was afraid she'd tell me (or I'd hear in her voice) that she thought I was wrong. That she was afraid I was making a mistake. Or that my choice wouldn't reflect positively on her. And then I'd be yanked from any connection with my own beliefs and desires, and I'd lose my footing and my conviction.

I'd learned that I desperately needed to sequester myself in a proverbial meditation cave when I was in a big life transition. Far away from anyone who thought they might know better. Especially my mom.

My mother, on the other hand, desperately wanted to be involved.

We couldn't both have what we needed. And I, like Barry, ultimately chose myself. It didn't feel *good,* but it felt, as my mother liked to say, *better than the alternative.*

So after my truncated visualization, she went through quite a long list of grievances she had about me and my behavior over the years. They mostly centered around this one topic — me not talking with her enough, not participating enough, and not making her feel important enough.

I could feel her grief through the phone. The cause of my repeated disappearances from her life didn't matter in this moment. What mattered was that we were talking, not screaming. Something felt different.

I listened to her list.

For each grievance, I apologized.

And for each grievance, she offered me forgiveness.

Right there on the phone, with me in the altered state she had gently guided me into, we took a giant step towards making peace.

It was as if God himself had hijacked the phone call.

19
Igan

We prepared the house for my mom, or as we now called her, Igan.

Her name, bestowed upon her by her only grandchild, was in perfect synchrony with her own relationship to words.

Words always had a special place in my mom's heart. To her, they weren't just tools, already forged, to be used in the construction of sentences. No, for her, words were malleable, soft, allowing. Beckoning to be altered.

Words morphed in my mother's presence.[4]

'Pregnant' became 'fragrant.'
'Bathroom' became 'thraboom.'
'Napkin' became 'nakrim.'

Words that needed emphasis were given extra suffixes. For example, something might be so incredible, that it was 'incredible-ness-tion-ful-ly.'

_____

[4] To see a more complete list of my mother's unique vocabulary, see the Glossary of Betty-isms in Appendix 3.

And, just to contradict herself perfectly, Mom was also a grammar snob.

"Did you actually just say, 'I wanted to lay down?'" she'd scoff. "Lie down," she'd correct me, looking down her nose and squinting her eyes like my fifth grade teacher used to do when she was about to tell us all to put our heads down for the remainder of class.

"Sorry, Mom. I'm tired," I'd say.

"Are you Deloris?" she'd quip, inserting one of her made-up words that meant 'delirious,' and totally missing the hilarious hypocrisy of the whole conversation.

But, in keeping with the holographic nature of all things, or, as my dad always says, "How you do *anything* is how you do *everything*," Mom and I also had tremendous fun with words.

We coined a new term—'disirregardlessly' to poke fun at the oft-used non-word 'irregardless.'

We deemed 'sweatpants' to be the placeholder for a word on the tip of your tongue that you just can't remember, as in, "I went to the Botanic Gardens yesterday and the...uh...*sweatpants* were in full bloom."

And I never got tired of hearing her tell the story of Anthony.

My mom was a former speech pathologist, and Anthony was a young boy she worked with at HeadStart—a community resource center for low income families.

Anthony wasn't exactly excited about learning from my mom. Each day they met, she would have flashcards and stories prepared. She'd have fun mouth yoga where he'd get to stick his tongue out at her, and make funny faces. But he wasn't so easily entertained. And he didn't give one rat's patootie about making 'proper' sounds.

"Pucker! Pucker! Puck you! Puck you!" is all he'd ever say.

Trying not to feed into his behavior, Mom would pretend she didn't hear his remarks, and she'd try to get him interested in fast cars and football.

"FFFFFootball."

"Puck you."

"FFFFFast car."

"Pucker! Pucker!"

This went on for weeks. But eventually, my mother's Christian upbringing collapsed, and she looked Anthony in the eye and said, "Anthony, watch my mouth. It's FFFFFFucker."

Whenever she told this story, she'd demonstrate Anthony's concentration on her own face. I could see him, through her, focusing so completely on the singular task of bringing his top teeth to rest just perfectly on his lower lip, arranging all those tiny muscles and aligning his entire being for this sacred word.

"FFFFucker!"

He did it.

She did it.

Together, they won.

Forty years after my mother's breakthrough with Anthony, when Felix was just getting a handle on language, Mom decided it was time to work her speech pathology magic on *him*. He'd already mastered the 'f' sound, so we weren't going to see Felix's cherubic face contorting around the word 'fuck.' No, it was 'Granny' she was hoping to coax out of him.

All three of us were playing in my backyard in California, running around in the wood chips and taking turns tossing a squishy ball back and forth.

Mom looked at me with those 'Here's my moment' eyes.

"Felix's turn," she said, pointing at him. He tossed the ball to her.

"Granny's turn," she said, pointing at herself.

He looked at her and giggled.

"Graaaanny," she said, pointing both hands back at herself.

He looked up at her with his impish grin and said, "Igan."

"Granny"

"Igan"

"Granny"

"Igan"

And on and on it went.

But finally she acquiesced. Igan it was. Once she accepted her new title, she puffed her chest out in pride and said, "Well, first there was the iPhone, then the iPod, then the iPad. Now there is iGan. I must be all the rage."

And now, eleven years and 2,500 miles away from that moment when iGan got her name, we prepared for her arrival.

My mom always had much higher standards for cleanliness than I did. Like, she would clean and I wouldn't. She used to tell me that I behaved like I was raised by wolves. Um. No, Mom. I was raised by *you.* But I certainly didn't act like it.

So, as you might imagine, getting ready for iGan was a bit of an ordeal. Dust monsters were captured and released into the wild. New towels were purchased because the washing machine lost the battle against the dirt stains in the old ones. The carcass of an old clothes dryer was carted out of the carport and hauled to the dump.

We had just painted the exterior of the house, so we were in luck there, except for the fact that we painted the house turquoise, which was definitely *not* on my mother's list of acceptable colors.

We also bought my mom a sleep mask to block out some of the blaring morning sunlight that would come into her peasant bedroom (the living room) and a white noise machine to ease the pain of the coqui frogs' mating song that plays on repeat all through the night.

We could never do it all right. I knew I had missed some crucial aspects to welcoming guests, and I knew I was going to hear all about them. But we did our hillbilly best.

20
Electric Peace

I was about halfway across the bay, looking around me for the familiar sight of those gorgeous gray fins.

And there they were.

There were about 50 of them. They surfaced in these graceful arcs, putting me in awe once again, and at the same time highlighting my awkwardness as a human.

Ten fins surfaced just a few feet away. I put my face in the water and saw their sweet faces coming towards me. I stopped kicking and just floated on the surface, trying not to move a muscle. One came up to me as if looking for a kiss, and then turned ever-so-slightly at the last moment, coming within half an inch of my face, keeping her eye on me as she passed.

I began to swim sideways, holding her gaze as we moved in unison at the surface of the water.

She began to dive.

I dove too.

We were about 10 feet down, smiling at each other. Pod members were above us, below us, twirling next to us.

There was a lot of activity, but inside my head there was utter silence. No words. No sounds. Not even my breath. We were moving slowly, eye-to-eye, in the deepest, most penetrating azure silence.

It was as if peace had become a liquid and we were suspended in it.

But this penetrating peace wasn't empty, or even still. It was dynamic, pulsating, electric.

Electric peace.

The place where your spirit dances freely because there is an abeyance of the internal war.

This wave of peace carried me for a good minute before I even thought to breathe.

I slowly surfaced, the dolphin rising with me, both of us, it seemed, enveloped in this dynamic, pulsating aliveness.

Maybe I had finally entrained to the dolphins — gotten my heart to beat in sync with theirs — and I was feeling the power of being a member of the pod.

Whatever that magic was, I vowed to carry it with me.

After that, the dolphins began to settle in to sleep. Diving deep, staying down longer, moving slower, gliding in unison.

They closed their eyes at the perfect moment, as it was time for me to return to my life on land. As the pod of 50 swam beneath me, I put my hands to my heart and said my thanks. A dolphin that was right beneath me at the time, in the middle of the serene pod, blew a toroidal bubble—a dynamic, swirling vortex ring that floated up towards me. I swam right above it and let it splash across my chest.

The electric peace of the spinners…
~photo by Lisa Denning

21
Late

I got a text message from Mom: "I'm going to be 8 HOURS late."

"Wha?"

"I overslept. Missed my flight that was supposed to leave at half past zero. Now I'm in for a 3-plane, 17-hour journey. But I'm on my way! I'll see you soon!"

Late? My mom was never late.

I take that back. My mom was always late, but she was never so late that she *missed* something. She was late for dinner, late to leave the house when she was meeting friends, late to take her walk, late to finish packing, late to fall asleep. But she never missed an appointment or an airplane. Ever.

My mom was the queen of planning. I'm sure she figured out the time she needed to leave for the airport, added an hour for her chronic tardiness, and put notes all over the house with the proper time of departure, along with lists of everything she needed to do in the morning before driving to the airport.

Her house was always littered with lists — grocery lists with, I kid you not, items organized by aisle; to-do lists for everything from 'clean out the garage' to 'make cookies' to 'make grocery list for making cookies.'

And she always 'packed on paper' before ever putting anything in her suitcase. She made lists of clothes to pack, clothes to wash, and clothes to purchase. When visiting me, she also made lists of recipes to bring, and even ingredients to pack, because my house is a culinary wasteland.

This time must have been a doozy. Not only did she need to bring gear for the ocean, but we had agreed to have an early Christmas celebration during her visit, and I, of course, owned nothing that even vaguely resembled a Christmas decoration.

Mom and I struggled with holidays, and Christmas in particular. She loved the togetherness, the festivities, the meticulous wrapping and voracious unwrapping of gifts. I despised the excessive materialism, familial obligation, and widespread chaos of the holiday season. I often complained that we had to celebrate this holiday *again*. Couldn't we skip a year? And Mom, of course, kept hoping I'd give in and enjoy it like every other normal human being.

This year was different. Mom was anxious to see us in our new home, and I guess she silently acknowledged that October was so close to December that it wasn't worth a fight to try and persuade us to fly out to Denver for the holidays. Instead, she packed an entire suitcase full of Christmas cheer—stockings to hang from the kitchen counter (no fireplaces here in Hawaii), wrapping paper, ribbon, cards, and even a few calligraphy pens to write notes to and from Santa.

Somehow, everything fit into two suitcases. And after 17 hours of travel, my mom arrived with all the necessary trappings for her week in hillbilly Hawaii. Within minutes of walking up the purple stairs and into the one big room that is our kitchen, living room, dining room, and guest room, she was snoring.

22
Christmas

Mom was still snoring as I crept past her to get to my home office the next morning. After my early calls, I went for my daily swim in the bay. Mom wanted to come with me, but she was still tired from her airplane ordeal, so she stayed home and got acquainted with Felix's latest creations and obsessions. He showed her his homemade fidget spinners made from skateboard parts and nylon cord, the butterfly knives he had constructed out of popsicle sticks, and then he serenaded her on his guitar.

By dinner, Mom was beaming. Spending time with Felix seemed to be as healing to her heart as it was to mine. Our love for him was one of the few things we always agreed on.

"Do you think we should do Christmas now?" asked Mom just before we sat down to eat.

Her spontaneity shocked me, as did the fact that she was interested in having our celebration before many of our gifts had arrived in the mail.

Hawaii has many luxuries, but swift package delivery isn't one of them. Receiving something within ten days is a major victory around here. None of us had fully adjusted to this new schedule, so many of our Christmas gifts were tardy for our excessively early celebration, but Mom didn't seem to care. She wasn't going to stand on ceremony this time, even if waiting a few more days would make the gift exchange complete.

"Yes!" I said. "Let's do it!"

We quickly wrapped the packages we did have, stuffed each others' stockings with the smaller items — 'neener' as my mother would say — and gathered in a sweet little circle on the floor like preschoolers getting ready to sing "The Days of the Week Song."

"Our celebration is today," Mom announced to all of us, "since we won't be together on Christmas."

I felt oddly sad when I heard her say that. Maybe my Grinch-ness was beginning to fade.

Felix played Santa, handing out the gifts. Most were directly from our wish-lists, since none of us could bear the pain of spending money on something that wasn't wanted, but there were a few surprises — items that had been carefully chosen by my parents, from their respective closets, for each other. My mom gave my dad a plaque that had been his father's, and that Mom had kept for 38 years. Dad, in turn, gave Mom a gorgeous framed photo of her playing the flute that he had taken of her when they were dating.

I don't have any memories of Christmas before my parents divorced, and I'd never seen them exchange gifts. Witnessing their connection and their kindness towards each other meant more to me than I ever thought it would.

"This might be a good visit after all," I thought, as the day came to a close.

Just before going to sleep, I climbed into bed next to Mom like I used to do when I was little. "Let's talk about today," she said, reminding me of our ritual as I was growing up.

"Today I got to be with your magical boy Felix," she said.

"And we didn't fight."

"And we had Christmas even though it isn't Christmas."

"And tomorrow we get to go swimming."

"And make candy cane cookies."

"G'night Maw. Thanks for coming all this way. I love you."

23
Judgment Day

I got into bed happier than I could have hoped for, but I couldn't sleep. I tossed and turned, got up, ate, tossed and turned some more, then finally gave up and ended up reading a marketing book in the bathroom with the lights on and the door closed — my attempt at quarantining myself in case this particular strain of insomnia was contagious.

There aren't any chairs in the bathroom, so I sat on the toilet. I often have to get up to pee in the middle of the night, so I wasn't just using the commode as a chair. I actually sat, drawers-dropped, on the pot all night long. I would read a page or two and pee. Another paragraph. More pee. A whole chapter this time. Pee.

The next morning, after no sleep and a lot of peeing, I felt an enormous, odd sense of relief. And no, it wasn't from all the peeing.

I felt *seen.* That type of seeing that makes you feel like, deep down, you're OK. That even if you flunk your test and don't get a date to prom and never make millions, you're still OK because your soul has been seen and accepted and validated. You've been looked at with piercingly observant eyes, deep into the abyss of who you are, where all your faults and quirks and oddities live, and despite all that, or maybe even because of it, you're loved.

I didn't often feel seen by my mom. I felt observed. Evaluated. Watched. And loved. But not *seen*.

Except when my alarm went off at 5:17 that morning, after a night of peeing but not sleeping, I *did* feel seen. And it was freaking me out.

It wasn't what I was expecting, or even what I thought I deserved. We had left Berkeley, CA, sold our house that was in an ever-increasing market, dropped our entire wad (proceeds from that sale plus my dad's life savings) into a two-unit house in the Hawaiian countryside, 20 minutes from a grocery store and 30 minutes from pretty much everything else.

It was Judgment Day.

But it wasn't.

I had created a life radically different from what my mom had envisioned for me, far away from all convention and all things I was supposed to do and be, and I had been accepted.

I scurried to get breakfast, tea, and down to my home office by 6 a.m. for my first business call of the day, but I stopped mid-oatmeal bite to talk with Mom. I felt an urgency to tell her of my relief, as if somehow talking about it was the last step in making it real.

"Mom, I have to tell you something."

"Yes?" She looked nervous. We often argued on the first few days of her visits.

"I didn't sleep last night. Like, *at all.* And I think I know why. Through the night I kept having this odd sense of relief, and I think it's because I don't feel judged by you. I was so scared you'd come here and judge everything. But you didn't. I've gotta run to my call. We can talk more after."

I leaned in for a quick hug, and then ran to get on the phone.

While I was on the phone, my parents talked, laughed, and had breakfast. Together. They hadn't spent this much time together in decades, and as I would learn later, they had a great time.

Maybe pigs *can* fly.

My dad likes to make what he calls 'The Abu' for breakfast—eggs and veggie burgers with cheese. It's a rather large meal, but he works up quite an appetite sorting nuts and bolts in his workshop all day.

As he tells the story, my mom was quite enthusiastic about joining him for this daily feast.

"Do you want eggs?"

"Yes!"

"Veggie burger?"

"Yes!"

"Cheese?"

"Yes!"

If my dad had offered scones and tea and chocolate, my mother would have said yes to those as well. She always was bigger on the inside than she ever was on the outside.

Back before I was even a thought in their minds, my parents used to host several of their friends each month for a grand orchestrated meal and celebration they deemed The Glutton of the Month Club, or the GOM.

They'd pick a theme, like all Moroccan food, or all blue food, and then they'd chop and blend and sauté like fools to create enough gourmet food that allowed 12 people to both overeat *and* have leftovers.

One month, the GOM members gave each other awards. My dad got Style. And I can see why. He has this elegance about him. Not because he spends excessive amounts of time or money on his appearance. No wingtip shoes or Armani suits. He's always in jeans and a t-shirt, but he emanates class. And he's hilarious.

My mother's award was Capacity.

So of course she wanted eggs and a veggie burger and cheese. I'm surprised she didn't eat my dad's portion too.

By the time I emerged from my home office, my parents had finished every last bite of the Abu masterpiece. They had also found some fins for my mom in our garage sale of a laundry room, so she was ready for the beach when I came up the stairs. It's a good thing, too, because I certainly didn't have the patience to help anyone with anything at that moment. 'Island time' had tapped me on the shoulder, but hadn't really settled in yet, and I was anxious to see the dolphins. They're more playful in the morning, and I was counting the minutes.

I quickly packed my snorkel gear and a bag of snacks for Mom and me to share after our swim. Not even the full Abu breakfast would keep Mom from being ravenous after an hour in the ocean.

We hopped in the car. The drive to the beach is only 2 miles. I bought a house that's 30 minutes away from civilization, and just 5 minutes from the beach. I've got my priorities straight. I still felt an urgency to discuss my relief with Mom, so I talked pretty much non-stop.

"I think I'm more confident now than I used to be," I said. "I'm in my element here, and I know it's where I'm supposed to be. I'm not trying to fit into a society that I don't belong in anymore. I wonder if I'm less prone to making up judgments. To feel them when they aren't intended. Sheesh, I wonder how much of that I've done over the years."

Mom looked at me with glassy, stunned eyes.

"And," I continued, "I really don't feel any judgment coming from you. I'm sure, with all that's happened, there are things that have been hard for you. You must have worked hard to make peace with what I've done. Thank you."

Finally, a smile.

"Yes, you're welcome. I have done a lot of work. Thank you for seeing it. For seeing me."

We pulled into the parking lot, and my attention was yanked from our heart-to-heart and out to those crystalline waters. We gathered our gear and walked down the path of tumbled stones to the little clearing where I stash my stuff each day.

"I'm talking a lot about myself this morning," I said. "Sorry."

"Sweetie, that's what I want. For you to let me in and tell me what's going on with you."

We put our rash guards on, and our swimming hats, and our booties, and got our snorkels all de-fogged and ready to go. Mom was putting on some of the strangest blue sunscreen I'd ever seen when I said to her, "You know Mom, when I imagined moving here, I always thought if I ever made it, I wouldn't want anything. That I'd be content. And the crazy thing is, it's true. This (as I pointed out to the ocean and the large pod of dolphins playing) is all I want."

"As a mom, that's all *I* want."

Time to get in.

"I climb on all fours," I said. "I see people trying to be fancy, but I've got no pride. Just ease your way down like this. You'll remember. You were here a few years ago. Once you start it will all come back to you."

Mom looked a little nervous, but she navigated the rocks like a champ. I helped her with her fins, and then she shooed me off to go be with my dolphin friends.

"Go ahead," she said. "Go play."

She knew the dolphins were my greatest love, and why I'd moved across the ocean. We had a plan to get in together and then meet on shore after an hour or so. My two-mile daily swim is a bit much for anyone else, even a five-time triathlete like her. She wanted to chill with the dolphins that were hanging out near the shore, and let me go get my yayas out by myself. Fair enough.

I swam off, played with the dolphins, then swam back and found Mom.

"Did you see them?"

"Yes!" she giggled.

I swam beneath her like a mermaid, and then helped her organize her swim hat and snorkel.

"Thanks, Boo," she said.

"Ooh, there they are!" I said, and swam off towards my finned friends.

24
Was

It was a beautiful swim. The dolphins were playful, the water was serene, and the sun was out. I was gone 30-40 minutes and I decided to head back to shore.

When I got back, strangers were poking around, looking at my stuff.

"Someone drowned," they said, "we're looking for ID."

"Oh gosh, I'm so sorry. That's my stuff."

"What about this?"

"That's my mom's."

"Do you know where your mom is?"

"No, but…"

"What was she wearing?"

"Long shorts."

"Pink top?"

"Yes."

"I hate to be the one to tell you, but it doesn't look good."

Then two policemen came over.

They helped me carry all the stuff I had brought to the beach—clothes, food, towels…for two.

The police escorted me to the hospital. One police car ahead of me, and one behind, while I drove my own car, praying, crying, screaming, pleading with any god that would listen.

"Please," I said. "Please let her be alive."

We parked where the ambulances park, and walked into the Emergency Room. As soon as I walked in, a nurse draped a warm towel over me.

I followed the policeman to the counter, guessing he was going to find out which room my mom was in, so I could go be with her while she recovered.

"What was your mom's name?" he said.

"Um. Betty. Her name *is* Betty Luellen-Clarke. Clarke with an 'e.'"

I heard his question—What *was* your mom's name?—but I couldn't take it in. I was trying to unhear that word, "was." If I didn't accept it, it wasn't true. These were the mind games I played with myself in order to stay upright.

The nurse then pointed me to a seat, and sat next to me. Despite the warm towels, I was shivering.

I was waiting to be told where to go, what my mom's condition was, how many tubes they had going into her body, and what they were doing for her.

"Where were you guys?"

"Kealakekua Bay. We were swimming with the dolphins."

"Was it rough?"

"No. Super calm today. Lots of people swimming and in kayaks."

"Yeah, I stopped off there on my way to work this morning," said another nurse. "Looked like a lake."

I couldn't bear it any longer.

"Is she alive?" I asked.

The nurse sitting next to me shook her head 'no.'

Tears.

Violent tears.

I tried to to weasel my way out of my reality. It can't be true. Don't they know how fit and healthy she is? How she was giggling just minutes ago? It doesn't make sense, so it can't possibly be true. Maybe if I can convince them of these things, they'll see...

"Do you want to see her?" said the policeman who first approached me at the beach. "Some people do and some don't."

"Oh, wait," said the other policeman. "We need you to identify her."

More warm towels.

They led me to the proper room. I walked in, still engaged in my personal cross-examination of what appeared to be happening.

And hoping it would be someone else lying on the table.

But there she was.

90

My mom.

Still.

Lifeless.

A tube for CPR in her mouth.

I screamed. Let out deep, guttural noises I didn't know I could make.

Then I wept. I hugged her. I stood at her side in disbelief.

How?

Why?

Was it really drowning like the man at the beach said?

She was a triathlete, having raced in open water just a few months before. More competent in the ocean than 90% of the people I see go in the bay each day.

Was it something else?

Did she have a heart attack?

Did she suffer?

Oh my God. What if she *did* drown?

I led my mom to her death.

I killed my mom.

I swam away and let her die alone.

I have done the worst thing anyone can ever do.

And I can't even say sorry. I can't make it better. I can't learn from this and do better next time.

There is no next time.

No next anything.

She's gone.

25
Demons

That night I was haunted by what I can only describe as demons. Ghosts. Visions of my mother hovering over my bed, pointer finger outstretched, screaming at me—"You didn't take care of me! You let me die! You didn't stay by my side! This is your fault!"

I would doze off for a few minutes, even an hour, then wake up in a frenzy—crying, kicking, punching, trying to escape my very skin. Somehow I felt like if I could succeed in clawing my way out of my body, time would reverse, events would alter, and I would not be where I was.

My mom said to me once, "Claire, I have decided that I cannot die because I do not want to put you through the pain I experienced when my mother died."

Now I understood why she said that. There was no pain I had felt that compared to the loss of my mother. It was like a connection to my very soul was severed.

After the kicking frenzy came the questions.

Why did she die?

Did she drown?

Did she have a heart attack?

Cardiac arrest?

Did she suffer?

Could I have saved her?

Did I really swim off and let her die?

26
Rick

Someone had to tell Rick. The police who escorted me to the hospital took down his home number, which is all I had, in an attempt to relieve me of that burden. But they couldn't get ahold of him.

I had my mom's cell phone, which he called from his cell mere hours after my mom died, but I missed the call. I tried to call him right back, but the phone locked up and I didn't know my mom's passcode. I tried to think of the most obvious codes she'd use, but honestly, I was relieved that I couldn't talk to Rick.

It was going to be the worst phone call of my life.

Rick was my mom's husband. The love of her life. The man she trusted her most intimate thoughts to. The man she traveled the world with. The man she chose to come home to every night.

He was also her high-school sweetheart.

Mom and Rick were married in 2006, but they met in 1963.

She was prom queen. He was on the football team. They were *that* couple.

Mom used to talk about Rick when I was growing up. How she knew they had to go their separate ways after high school, and how they probably wouldn't have been a good match to raise children together, but she still cared for him.

So when I was about 17 months pregnant and my mom called to tell me she was seeing someone and "this time it's different," I wasn't surprised to learn that it was Rick.

Far from the aspiring football star she dated in high school, Rick was now a retired physician who had spent the last several decades in some of the most conservative areas of the country. My mother, being a diehard liberal, warned me of this, but said, "Give him a chance. He's a good man."

I met Rick at my baby shower. He flew out with my mom to meet me, my husband, and my belly. When the two of them walked in my house, I was struck with how different my mom was. Something had been sparked in her. Something good. Something I'd never seen before.

I was going to have to get used to Rick.

My mom was nervous about this relationship. Not because it wasn't good, but because it was *too good.* She had lived alone for so long. And her only marriage had ended in divorce.

But that didn't stop Rick.

After two years, he proposed.

She turned him down.

After another six months, he proposed again.

Nope.

"Okay," he said. "Next time *you* have to propose to *me*."

It only took 2 months.

He accepted.

They had ten years together, and while I had plenty of polite (for me) conversations with Rick during that time, we never really talked about anything *real.*

I had no foundation with him, except what I borrowed from my mom. He was her husband. That was our only connection.

Until now.

We were about to be connected in the deepest, darkest way, through grief.

The thought of calling Rick collapsed my throat, my chest, and made it almost impossible to breathe.

"He's going to hate me," I thought.

"He's going to believe, like I believe, that this was my fault."

Of all the future moments my mother was supposed to be alive, the vast majority were supposed to be spent with Rick. It was *his* life, even more than mine, that was going to be impacted by my mother's premature passing.

My demons grew with these thoughts, as I kept trying to find Rick, but kept hoping I wouldn't.

In the end, I didn't have to tell him.

I found my aunt, who found Rick's sister, who found Rick while he was driving home from his fishing trip. He was 15 minutes away from home when the call came in, and his entire family was waiting at the house by the time he arrived, having flown in from all over the country in the 24 hours we had been searching for him.

I just knew they were all talking about how I, my mother's unruly and impossible child, had stolen her from this Earth.

My phone rang.

It was Rick's sister's phone number.

My heart began to race as I picked up the phone.

"Hello?"

"Hello, Claire. It's Rick. This isn't your fault."

27
Grace

The grace with which Rick spoke to me that day was stunning. I was speechless. I blubbered and wailed into the phone, trying to take in the fact that *he was on my side.*

I was grateful. And relieved. But in many ways I didn't believe him. Neither did my demons. They refused to just lie down and die with one man's proclamation that I was innocent. Not even if it was Rick.

The only thing that did have a chance of easing my pain was, ironically, the ocean.

As I packed my bags to go to the beach, I had the sense that I was breaking the law, or breaking tradition, or at the very least breaking convention. I was willingly going right back to the scene of the crime, so to speak. I was, on purpose, putting myself right back in the exact waters that stole my mother's life.

I drove down the hill, not feeling connected to my body or my surroundings. It was as if I was watching a shell of myself turn the steering wheel.

When I arrived, I expected to be plunged back into the trauma of the day before. Pain. Shock. Tragedy. Doom.

Strangely, the ocean greeted me with peace, as if it was just another day. I walked slowly down the tumbled rocks to the shore, as I had done every day since we moved to the island.

The water was just as serene as the day before.

And I could see the dolphins playing in the distance.

My memory flashed from the day before, when my mom was expertly navigating the rocks with me.

"She's supposed to be here with me today, too," I said in my head.

My eyes welled up as I took those last steps into the water. I put my face in, felt the rush of the cool, silky water, and I felt the tiniest bit better.

And then I saw it. Right in front of me, hanging in the water, was a perfect heart. A leaf in the shape of a heart, staring at me. It was perfectly intact except for one hole in the upper left-hand corner, as if someone had taken a hole-punch and cut a circle in the left ventricle.

How fitting.

But I didn't feel pain at the sight of the leaf. Rather, I sensed my mom, sending her love. She knew I'd come right back to these waters. She knew I'd get in right here. She knew I'd receive her heart emoticon from the other side.

Thanks, Mom.

I plucked the heart from the ocean, and did the most sacred thing I could think of — I placed it directly on my left butt cheek, made sure it was held in place with the drawstring on my bikini bottoms, and told my mom and whoever else was listening that I would retrieve it at the end of my swim. (Which I did. I later took it home, dried it, laminated it, and put it in the drawer by my bed. It's now my favorite bookmark.)

Feeling complete with my leaf-clad buttocks, I swam out to meet my friends.

Just like the ocean, they too seemed unaffected by my mom's departure. Both as peaceful and as exuberant as ever, they swam around me, underneath me, and jumped in gorgeous arcs above me.

Believing fully in their wisdom and their connection with Spirit, I began to plead:

What happened to my mom?

Why?

Where is she?

Was it my fault?

Silence.

Not just silence as in the dolphins didn't squeak and click out the answers to my questions. But true silence, just for a moment, in my head.

What a welcome respite.

Then these words came, and not from me. Not from my incessant mind chatter. Not from my aching heart. They came from the dolphins. From the Universe. From God.

> *Don't search for answers.*
> *You will be taken care of.*

Then a young dolphin came right up to me, looked me in the eye, bobbed his head up and down like a puppy asking to play fetch, and I was back to the physical world.

My mom always loved the water. And she never missed a moment to be silly, or to tell a joke.

Whenever we would go to the swimming pool or the ocean, she'd do this silly, acrobatic twirling maneuver. It was her signature parody of synchronized swimming.

Lying on her back, toes straight up in the air, holding herself up with the swiftest and most adept hand motions, she'd twirl. First in a circle, keeping her head as the center, and her body as the twirling radius, and then she'd add barrel rolls. Like the Earth orbiting the Sun, she was an utterly goofy twirling baton, circling nothing.

Sometimes I'd join her in her water dance, and we'd spin in unison until we laughed so hard we couldn't hold ourselves up any longer.

So here came this young dolphin, obviously wanting my attention. He bobbed his head and wagged his tail some more until he was sure I was watching, and then he flipped over on his back. His white belly facing up, his tail still, he wiggled his flippers and proceeded to transform himself into the twirling baton that I knew so well. He skipped the elementary step, going straight for the barrel roll and orbit-of-nothing. There he was, a teenage dolphin, performing my mother's synchro routine.

I didn't know whether to laugh or cry, so I did a sort of gasp-hiccup, brought my hand to my mouth, let the left corner of my mouth curl up in a smirk just broad enough to fill my mask with water, and peed.

28
Surrender

I was right about the ocean. It did make me feel better. It eased my pain enough that I felt almost human for a few hours before the demons began their chanting in my head again. Their tormenting words were the loudest in the middle of the night and in the wee hours of the morning, waking me up and yanking me out of whatever dream I had briefly escaped into.

This is how the next several days would go. I'd wake up at 3:00 or 4:00, or on the lucky days at 5:00, thrashing about in my bed, punching and kicking the vengeful ghosts that stalked me. After an hour or so, the battle would eventually subside, only to be replaced with a heaviness that pinned me to my mattress. I'd lie there for a few hours, paralyzed, wondering if I'd ever regain control over my limbs.

I always did.

Bit by bit, my muscles would come online and begin responding to my requests for movement. Eventually my body and I would sync up enough to make tea, eat a papaya, and pack my bags for the beach. And each day, the ocean would graciously grant me a few hours of peace.

As for the other 20 or so hours of the day, I was back to wrestling guilt.

As I fought this colossal demon each day and night, I kept hearing the word, "surrender." I knew I was losing the battle against whatever I was fighting, but I didn't know what else to do.

Surrender to what?

And how?

I would wake up in the middle of the night, kicking and sobbing. My legs doing the bicycle under the covers, trying to escape my body, my reality, the fact that my mother had died in my beloved waters.

"Surrender," it kept saying.

But I still kept fighting. Resisting. Looking for a doorway that would lead me out of the pain that was my new existence. I ate and breathed pain. It was my new, prickly, heavy, dangerous world.

"Surrender," it said.

Surrender.

To what?

Death?

Was I supposed to let my pain engulf me? Was I to drown in guilt as a punishment for allowing my mother to drown in the ocean?

Surrender.

I had the physical strength to bicycle through the night, but I didn't have the emotional strength to resist or hide my guilt. I couldn't even find the sadness I felt over losing my mom. The guilt was so overbearing.

Surrender.

The pain would come in tsunami-like waves, destroying everything in their path.

The truth is, I had no choice but to surrender, whatever that meant.

Was it supposed to happen?

Was it her time?

Did I know?

Was it the disturbance in the proverbial Force that kept me up the night before?

Did I know I only had a few hours that morning to make peace?

Is that why I felt such urgency?

Did *she* know?

Is that why she brought my father something of *his* father's that she'd had for decades?

Is that why, for the first time in her life, she bought travel health insurance?

Is that why, a month previous, when she and I had a strange but heated argument, she finally broke down and said, "I'm just *used up*, Claire."?

Is that why she left her last wishes — burial preferences, location and type of funeral — hand-written on her desk at home? Not neatly typed and stapled to her extensive will that outlined every valuable item in the house. Not placed in a manila folder and filed away under "last wishes." No, this list was handwritten on a yellow legal pad as if she'd scrawled it in haste the night before her flight.

It gave me pause.

"Bear paws?" my mom would have said.

Yes, Mom. Large, furry, menacing paws.

Did you know?

Do we *all* know?

Is this one of the great secrets — that we all receive a cosmic text message near the hour of our death, letting us know what's coming and giving us just enough time to clean and patch old wounds?

Surrender.

I decided that the one thing I could truly surrender to was pain.

I couldn't make any of it OK, but I could stop resisting the hellish reality that I was now in. So I sat. And breathed. And welcomed, as best I could in my feeble state, the volcanic eruptions of grief.

I let myself be consumed. Overtaken. Devoured.

I once watched a National Geographic film where a cheetah was chasing its prey — a deer or antelope or some other cute hooved creature. As an extreme empath and a lover of the underdog, I was rooting for the deer, but, alas, he was caught.

I could hardly watch, but what I saw gave me the spiritual lesson that I so desperately needed in this moment of grief.

The deer ran as fast as he could, for as long as he could. And once he was caught, he tried to free himself. But when it became clear, however these things become clear, that he was not going to escape, he calmly let go. He surrendered to his own death.

Did the deer know something about the afterlife that we don't know? Did he know he was going to take a brief respite in the lounge of the void and quickly return to Earth as his next incarnation? Or did he just calmly accept *nothing forever* as his next place of residence?

Whatever the reason, he surrendered to what we might call the most terrifying and devastating of all things — death by mauling.

I needed to become that deer.

To relax into my own dismemberment.

So I breathed.

And allowed myself to be devoured.

It was excruciating.

But it was not endless.

Each time the pain came up, I learned to breathe, to almost relax, to let it overtake me, and then to let it pass.

When I didn't fight it, it would actually pass.

It would return (still does) but it would pass.

And I would emerge, post-mauling. Wounded, but very much alive.

29
Peace

Interspersed between the hours of anguish, were moments of peace. Deep peace.

Enveloping, all-consuming, every-cell-of-my-body peace.

Somehow, for brief periods of time, I was being slammed into the present moment.

The finiteness of life was staring me in the face, saying, "All we have is a string of moments just like this one. Pay attention."

The peace was always sandwiched between a pain so intense I wasn't sure I could survive it. The possibility, however small, that I had contributed to my mother's death created a monster inside of me.

The pain was so big, so consuming, so suffocating, I literally thought it might kill me.

So did my dad. He took me aside one day and said, "Claire, we can't lose TWO. Don't let this break you."

But I was already broken.

And yet, somehow, in my brokenness, or perhaps because of it, something seeped into my being.

Peace.

Presence.

Something otherworldly.

I might even say a glimpse of divinity snuck in the crack in my soul.

A dear friend of mine misquoted Rumi to me during that time of utter brokenness: "Perhaps there is no difference between heart-break and heart-opening," he said.

I was, without a doubt, broken. If that meant my heart was opening, allowing for the Peace of God to seep in, then I would welcome it with arms as wide as I could manage. When they weren't clenched in fists attacking my pillow, or clutching a soft blanket filled with tears and snot, I would open my arms to this peace.

30
Filiz

As I walked the familiar path along the beach, I saw my friend Filiz.

"Hi Filiz."

"Hi Claire."

"Asularia says you were there with my mom."

"Yes, I helped carry her to shore. And to take off her fins and booties."

"Thank you...So you saw her?"

"Yes. The dolphins were here. We were all swimming with them."

"You saw her swimming?"

"Of course."

"Do you know what happened?"

"She was swimming, and then, all of a sudden, she stopped swimming. We carried her to shore. There were several people helping — a fireman, a doctor — all tourists here for the dolphins. I was certain she'd make it because we got to her so soon. I'm so sorry, Claire."

"Thank you Filiz. Thank you."

And then she gave me the warmest hug.

I immediately texted Rick: "She said my mom was swimming, and then all of a sudden, she stopped swimming."

He wrote back: "Sounds like a medical event!"

And then I got in the water, feeling the eensiest bit better. Maybe she didn't suffer after all.

When I returned home, Rick called. "After your text," he said, his voice cracking, "I was inspired to call the hospital. I spoke with the doctor who did the autopsy. I asked him what they found, saying the family would find peace in knowing she didn't suffer. But he said, 'Dr. Clarke, I wish I could tell you that. But I can't.'"

"So we'll never know?" I asked.

"We'll never know."

31
EMDR

Buzz... buzz... buzz...

Every few seconds, this device buzzed in one of my hands. First my left hand, then my right. The buzzing alternated this way throughout the entire session.

I was receiving one of the many forms of EMDR (Eye Movement Desensitization and Reprocessing), a therapeutic approach that is designed to reduce the effects of Post Traumatic Stress Disorder (PTSD), which is what I had been told I was suffering from. I thought PTSD was reserved for war veterans and rape victims, but apparently any cataclysmic event that creates loops in the brain that replay an exquisite horror can be classified as PTSD.

Well, I certainly had loops.

Sometimes the movie that played in my head was of me emerging from the ocean onto the rocky shore. Sometimes I'd be swimming back to meet my mom, but I knew I'd meet the police instead. Mostly though, I would be entering the hospital room where my mom's warm but lifeless body lay. I'd shriek, and thrash around, trying to escape the scene. And then the 10-ton weight of responsibility would descend on my chest and restrict my breathing.

This... was... my... fault.

Buzz...

In EMDR, you connect with a positive resource to help you through these loops. And, ideally, these resources assist you in taking the charge off of the event. You don't lose your memory, but the trauma fades.

Your resource is supposed to be something or someone that brings you peace, helps you to relax, and to feel taken care of. Oddly enough, my resources were actually present during the very event I was attempting to desensitize myself to.

Anne, my therapist, asked me to describe the scene that was looping in my mind, and then told me to call in my resources. Instantly I was back in the water, in the bay, with the dolphins.

Buzz…

But instead of just swimming and playing, I was carrying what looked like an iridescent windowpane. It was about 6 feet by 4 feet, and it shimmered like the rainbow surface of an oil spill in an asphalt-paved parking lot.

As soon as I got close to the dolphins with my windowpane, it shattered.

Buzz...

It looked like glass splintering into a thousand pieces, but instead of the pieces crashing into the water, they simply vanished.

Buzz…

"It's an illusion. They tell me it's an illusion. The dolphins tell me my guilt is an illusion."

Buzz…

"And it cannot survive in their presence, so my windowpane shatters.

I'm not in charge of everything, they say.

I don't decide when someone's ready to go, they say.

Surrender, they say."

Buzz…

"Wait, I'm back in the water with my mom. She's there. She's fine. I'm going to stay with her this time. 'Is that okay?'" I ask Anne.

"Yes, you can say or do whatever you're guided to do."

Buzz…

"It doesn't change things. If I stay with my mom. If I don't swim away, the outcome is the same."

"For her?"

"Yes. She still dies."

32
Funeral

The funeral was at the Botanic Gardens. Rick first tried to book the City Park Pavilion, overlooking my mom's favorite view — City Park Lake, but the first opening was October 30th, and I told him by that point I'd probably lose my interest in attending the service, so we went for the Botanic Gardens.

You see, I have a history of not attending gatherings, ceremonies, and other family events. They injure my introvert. Rick understands this better than most, which is quite remarkable considering his own extroverted tendencies.

So the two of us decided on the Botanic Gardens. My mom deemed herself a gardening fool, taking any chance she could to plant and cultivate something beautiful in her yard. In fact, one of her favorite Christmas gifts from me in recent years was a headlamp that allowed her to garden at night.

To both my mother's chagrin and amusement, I did not share her love of botanical grooming. She often liked to recall the time when, as a child, I was pulling weeds as one of my household chores. She walked over to admire my work, and asked me how it was going. I looked up at her with a surly preteen face and said, "Just kill me now."

Despite the chasm between my mother's world and mine, we did have moments of perfect synchronicity. One time, during one of our many moves, my mom was staying at Many Mansions—an extended stay hotel—while I spent a few weeks with my dad. I visited Mom at her temporary abode, and we were having dinner on the little terrace, overlooking the busy 17th Avenue in downtown Denver. During a moment of culinary acrobatics, I mistakenly flung a piece of asparagus over the edge of the terrace and onto the street below. Instead of sparking an argument between the sloth (me) and the gourmand, we both erupted into fits of giggles. Soon after the giggles began, we started to sing… "There's asparagus on somebody's tiiiiiiiiire." For decades to come, that line would find itself in our conversations. A moment of utter sillitude and complete connection.

Oddly enough, the choosing of my mom's funeral location was another moment of synchronicity. For the celebration of my life, I'd be most honored if everyone stayed home and did their favorite silent activity in tribute to me. But not my mom. I knew she'd want loads of people, dressed pristinely, gathered in what she considered one of the most beautiful places on Earth—a flower garden. I was sure of this. Rick was sure of this. And later, once it was all booked and paid for, Rick found the handwritten note on my mother's desk with her funeral wishes. City Park Pavilion & Botanic Gardens were the top two on the list.

This day was dedicated to my mom—her life and her loves—so hundreds of us met at the Botanic Gardens.

At the entrance, we were greeted with a huge display of colorful skulls, skeletons, and a banner that read "Special Day of the Dead Performance" with an arrow pointing to the left. I laughed, thinking they nailed my mom's sense of humor, and began to pivot left.

"It's this way, Claire," directed Rick, pointing to a tiny sign taped beneath the display that said "Celebration of Life for Betty Luellen-Clarke" with an arrow to the right.

Ah yes, the big display was in honor of the Mexican holiday that comes right after Halloween. Not for my mom's funeral. Or maybe Mom was playing with us all.

We found our way to the proper venue. It was appropriately gorgeous. And in the shade. My mom would approve.

There was a line of people waiting to get in, as if it were some rock concert. Katy was at the entrance, handing out programs, smiling just the right amount for such an occasion—not too much as to seem actually happy, but not too somber either, knowing that even the slightest head nod, or downward gaze could catalyze a train of infectious tears that we were all attempting to put at bay for at least another few minutes.

As I moved closer to the front of the line, I saw Katy catch a glance of me. Both her head and her eyes dropped. She couldn't help it. Her mouth just wouldn't smile. Not even one of those fake smiles that we all learn on picture day at school.

My turn.

"Hi Claire, I'm Katy. I took the pictures of…"

"I know. Thanks. They're beautiful."

"We all loved your mom so much."

"I know."

This is how so many of my conversations would go. People telling me their names as if I'd forgotten. Reminding me of who they were, as if I had no memory of when I was a child. The truth is, they hadn't changed much — an extra pound here, an extra wrinkle there. It's me who'd changed. I wasn't the little girl they remembered, so maybe they thought that they must be equally unrecognizable.

The service was beautiful. As much as a funeral can be a celebration, it was.

After the last speaker, the inevitable line formed. Everyone wanted to talk with me and Rick. We were sitting next to each other in the front row, so two lines formed, but at some point they came together, forming a snake tongue that seemed to extend into Nevada.

After about 20 minutes, I began to feel light-headed. I don't think I'd been fully in my body since emerging from the water that fateful day my mom and I went out for a swim, but this was bordering on faint.

The line continued. One person would come to me, say their 'I'm sorrys' and 'I loved hers' and 'she loved yous' and as they left, the next person would appear, as if an endless Pez dispenser was feeding me mourner after mourner.

After all those hugs, I began to smell like the foyer at Macy's, where a woman is offering perfume samples. Not just their favorite, or their best seller. But a smorgasbord to choose from.

I had been slimed by every perfume, cologne, and cosmetic product for miles. And decades.

So there I was, light-headed and nauseous, looking out at the never-ending snake tongue of a line, when an angel appeared. Not an otherworldly being with wings. No. A person. But an angel nonetheless.

Her name is Barbara and she wore a white and pink dress with big crocheted flowers on the front, and a hat she had set slightly askew on her head.

"Hello Darling," she said as she took my hand. She put her other hand on my shoulder, and then, in all of her five foot three stature, she shielded me from the snake.

With Barbara leading the way, we made our way to the back of the venue, where there was a glorious display of food. Fruits and vegetables of all colors, meats, my grandma's recipe of candied pecans, and a silver swan-shaped bowl with a delicate ladle for dispensing chocolate sauce. I think the sauce was intended as an accessory to the fruit, but I could hear my mother, reaching across the veil, whispering to all of the passersby that *everything* is better when drenched in chocolate.

Barbara put a plate of food together for me, reminding me that even daughters mourning their mothers need to eat. We sat down on some concrete benches, and my SortaMom Anita came over. Barbara started to shoo her off, but I said Anita was allowed. She knew how to sit

124

with me in silence and protect me from the throngs of my mother's friends.

Shaking, I slowly brought the fork to my mouth. I couldn't really taste anything, but I was grateful for the calories. I almost felt present.

Barbara leaned in so only I could hear her, and said, "Your mama's heart failed her."

It was as if the cave I had imprisoned myself in *cracked* at that moment. A sliver of moonlight crept in and illuminated a single drop of water on the cave floor.

Barbara is an intuitive. A brilliant, gifted-beyond-belief intuitive.

She knew I was going to be a writer when I was still hell-bent on becoming a surgeon. She knew the year I would marry, and that it wouldn't be to the man I was asking about at the time. She knew exactly the parenting style my son would need as a teenager when he was just a wriggling pollywog in my womb.

And today she was telling me, in a way I could finally hear, that I wasn't at fault for the death of my mother.

I almost smiled.

For the rest of the service, for the eternity of the after-service gathering at my mom's house. Through dinner, and through all of the conversations with the mourners from the snake tongue that I left in the dust at the Botanic Gardens. Through all that, I almost smiled.

33
Thank You

I pulled into the parking lot of Kealakekua Bay Park, piled my 3 bags on my shoulders, and walked over to the water.

Huge waves today. And not just waves. Turbulence. Chaos. Unpredictable swells. Of course, the chaos and the unpredictability were only in my head. A real shaman of the sea would see the patterns. She would be able to speak to the ocean. To ask permission to enter. And she would be guided in at the perfect moment.

I was not that attuned.

So I went back to my car and headed down what my mother called 'The Road to Nowhere.' It's a narrow road with barren lava rock on either side, giving you the appearance you're sightseeing on Mars. It feels like a fairly spacious one-lane road until you see someone coming the other way and you realize that, somehow, two cars must fit. The edges of the road fall off at sharp angles, sometimes it's a completely vertical drop, and I'm always afraid I'm going to topple over the edge and get stuck in the ditch forever.

Of course, it never happens. There's always just enough space for both cars to squeak past each other, as long as no one breathes during the passage.

I went down this road because it leads to my second favorite swimming spot—Pu'uhonua o Honaunau. Or as we locals affectionately call it, Two Step. Two Step is sheltered from the winds and swells, it's sunnier there, and there are literally two steps that you walk down to enter the ocean. In fact Two Step has two sets of two steps to assist you into the sea.

Two Step was obviously the safer option today. I parked on the side of another tiny, treacherous feeling road, walked down to the slab of lava rock that we call a beach, and saw that I had, indeed, made the right choice.

Not only was it sunny and calm, but a pod of about 40 dolphins were circling 50 yards from shore.

I got my gear on, walked down my preferred set of steps, and plunged into my second favorite playground.

I could hear the clicks and squeaks of the dolphins singing, and within a few short minutes I was playing the leaf game with a small group of enthusiastic spinners.

One breath in, one breath out. Two breaths in, and out. I took a third breath in and held it, diving about 20 feet down. Two teenage dolphins with their bright eyes and smiling faces watched as I placed a leaf in front of them. One gave the head-bob of acknowledgement and the other opened his mouth and playfully took the leaf in his teeth. He shook his head back and forth a few times, then opened his mouth and let the leaf float back and fold around his dorsal fin.

He looked over at me, playfully opened his mouth, shook his head like he did when first picking up the leaf, and then slowly circled me, keeping my gaze. As usual, I squeaked and smiled so big that my cheekbones pushed my mask off-center and it began to fill with water. I, of course, didn't care.

The dolphin then dropped the leaf next to me and swam off to reconnect with his pod. I picked it up and put it in my favorite 'pocket' right on my left butt cheek.

"Thank you," I called out softly. "Thank you for letting me join in your sweet dolphin games."

The pod swam off faster than I could follow, but they were circling in a fairly small bay, so I knew they'd be back shortly. I picked my head up, pulled off my mask, and looked around for the glistening fins.

Instead of fins, I saw a familiar human face. It belonged to a man who appeared to be clinging to a boogie board for dear life, holding a GoPro. It had to be Jim."

Jim is a friend of mine from California. A brilliant man, my former business coach, and almost-business-partner.

"Hi Jim!" I shouted.

"Hi Claire," he responded nonchalantly, as if it's totally normal to bump into your old friends while floating in the Pacific with a pod of dolphins.

"Claire!" I heard Shellie, his girlfriend. She wasn't so nonchalant, swim-running over to me with arms wide open. We hugged until it became clear we were going to sink unless we got our arms back involved in treading water, and we began to squeal like little children at our happenstance meeting.

We bantered a few niceties back and forth and then quickly moved to the topic of my mom. Shellie is a professional intuitive and spiritual counselor, and she's very interested in the comings and goings of souls from the Earthly plane.

"So, she was visiting you."

"Yeah. And we were swimming with the dolphins, just like this. I followed a pod across the bay, and when I came back, she was gone."

"What happened?"

"I don't know. Someone found her floating. At first we all thought she drowned."

Shellie shook her head 'no.' She was tapping into something.

"But I'm not sure that makes sense." I continued. I wished I would just shut up and let Shellie tell me what she was seeing or feeling, but I had that nervous-speak thing going where I couldn't seem to stop the runaway train that was my story.

On and on I went… "it could have been her heart…" Shellie nodded 'yes.'

"Do you want me to tell you what I'm getting?" she asked.

"Yes, of course," I said (and thank you for shutting me up.)

"She's saying thank you. 'Thank you, thank you, thank you, Claire.'"

I couldn't quite fathom why, but I did my best to take it in.

34
One Not Two

At some point, I began to move away from the intense pain, and to turn towards a thought so foreign to me that I was amazed it made it through the security of my psyche.

I began to toy with the idea that my mother's death had not, in fact, broken me. I began to see how I was, despite my heartache, becoming *more whole*.

I had given in so completely to the pain, and it hadn't killed me. Somehow, it seemed to be knitting pieces of me together. Pieces that never played well together before. Pieces that used to give me stomach aches and keep me up at night. It was as if the tragedy of my mother's sudden and untimely death had caused the warring parts of me to come together for a greater cause, like nations can come together against a common enemy.

It was an odd place to be headed.

Wholeness.

The demons began to fade. They no longer hovered over my bed or pointed their fingers at me.

Decisions became easier. Big decisions, like which of my mom's possessions I should keep (and ship the 3,300 miles from Denver to Kona.) And small decisions, like whether to put a comma in a sentence or not. They all became easier.

The orchestra of voices that used to come out and parade around my mind had vanished. There was a singular voice left, and it wasn't the monkey mind. Not the endless mind chatter that narrates your entire life, and snarks at everything walking by (at least that's how mine worked.) No, the only voice left was the voice of my gut. My connection to Self, the Universe, Spirit.

Yogic philosophy says you can reach enlightenment by meditating on one short mantra — "One. Not two." — because you'll arrive at the truth of non-duality and oneness. I certainly hadn't attained enlightenment, but I didn't have two voices anymore — what I wanted and what I thought I should want — but rather one singular voice that knew what was true…*for me*. An intuitive signal in my gut that gave me answers to questions and problems my brain could never solve.

Maybe this was the na'au.

35
That Feeling Is You

Years ago, before I called this island home, and before I became so spoiled with ocean miracles that I could go a day or even a week without seeing my finned friends and not feel cheated by the universe, I was out searching for dolphins. I had hopped in the water at the pier in town, and was swimming alongside paddle boarders, surfers, and tourist boats.

I had braved the chaos of town because it was my last day here. I was desperate. My two favorite aquatic playgrounds had been void of cetaceans the entire time I was visiting, and I was panicking. So instead of being persistent and checking out the bays again on this last day (which, I found out later, would have delivered exactly what I wanted, since a large pod was at Two Step that day) I drove to town and swam out from the pier.

After about a half-mile swim, I got this feeling in my chest—a warm, giddy feeling that I get when the dolphins are near. I had never felt this way *without* the dolphins, so I figured they were close by, and I was going to hear their squeaks and see their smiling faces any minute.

But they didn't appear.

Instead, I heard, "That feeling you have in your heart...That's YOU. That's Claire."

Nai'a Healing was based on that premise — that it's a connection with yourself that you're missing, and that when you re-establish it, and line your life up with who you really are, you heal. I had spent years connecting people to the small voice within, and helping them rearrange their lives to align with it.

But somehow I couldn't take my own advice. I could be the land dolphin for everyone else, but I held on to the idea that *I* needed the *real* dolphins. The marine dolphins. The ones with dorsal fins and sonar.

As I felt the disparate pieces of myself begin to knit together, I thought back to that time in the ocean when I was reminded that the magic to heal comes from within.

And possibly for the first time, I listened.

In the presence of the dolphins, I feel nothing but love. A love so large, so soft, so nurturing, so overwhelming, that it fills all available space. My mind fills with this love. My heart fills. My eyes and ears and nose and toes fill. And when I'm submerged in this ocean of love, I become unencumbered with the thoughts of being less-than, and I can connect to my deepest Self. The Self that knows what's true and right and healing, *for me.*

Love. That's the healer.

Grief, too, is a manifestation of love.

When the grief over my mother wasn't wrapped in daggers of guilt and shame, it was the greatest expression of love I'd ever experienced.

Nearly every spiritual tradition across the globe says that at our core, we are love. The challenge of the spiritual quest isn't to fundamentally alter who you are, but rather to break down the stone walls that are the false self so that you can become acquainted with who you've always been.

My experience told me that once you meet your truest self, and accept her in all her glorious imperfection, a door opens. A door that, if you dare to enter it, can lead you to wholeness.

When my heart opened in the presence of the dolphins, I grinned and cooed and my snorkel mask filled with water. When my heart opened in grief, I keened and moaned and kicked. But ultimately I surrendered.

And when I ran my white flag up the pole and stopped resisting the avalanche of love that was attempting to infiltrate my heart in the form of grief, I found that it, too, had a healing effect.

I became more connected to myself. I became more connected to my mother. And I became more whole than ever before, having been broken and reassembled by my grief.

Love won.

36
Ho'o'ponopono

Ho'o'ponopono is a Hawaiian forgiveness process. It used to be done in person, mediated by a shaman, and could take days. Each party would lay down their arms, so to speak. Their defensive arguments. Their egos. Their need to be right. They would forgive the other for whatever wrongdoing had been committed, and ask for forgiveness for their own part. Even if the 'fault' seemed to fall clearly on one person's shoulders, both parties would both forgive and ask for forgiveness.

'Ho'o' means 'to make' and 'pono' means 'right.' So Ho'o'ponopono means to make right twice. To make aligned twice. To make pono twice. Today, it is mostly practiced as an energetic process—one you do in your own mind.

Years ago, when I first learned the Ho'o'ponopono technique—how to invite people onto the stage in my mind, to give and offer forgiveness, and to cut the 'aka cords'—the energetic connections that keep old hurts alive—my mind wandered to a time when I had done something forbidden. Something both illegal and taboo.

Tapping into my Wild Woman as my mom called her, I hiked to the edge of Kilauea, the active volcano here on the Big Island. I went with a local who said he did it regularly, and, as my mom often reminded me, I can be too trusting. So I went.

The hike wasn't really a hike at all. It was a walk. A jaunt. A saunter. There was a paved road all the way to the crater, and there was even an area with ropes, like you see in a museum or crowded movie theater, so people could stand in line to get their moment *right at the edge*. The end of the line was just a few feet from the half-mile wide crater that was sloshing and churning with molten rock. I guess there was a time when this wasn't taboo.

I was mesmerized. I could hear the ocean waves, crashing on the shore... Except that they weren't ocean waves and they weren't crashing on the shore. They were lava waves, and they were crashing on the inside of the crater.

I felt like I was at the heart of creation itself, and I offered my gratitude, my humility, and a bunch of bananas to Pele, the goddess of the volcano. I tossed the bananas into the crater, and a spout of lava came shooting up in the air. I took that as Pele's thanks, and then I just stood there, staring at the giant vat of liquid rock, for two solid hours.

As I sat in class, learning about Ho'o'ponopono and its importance in the Hawaiian culture, I knew I had to confess to my teacher what I had done. So on our next break, I approached him.

"Kumu, I have a question…"

"Yes, Claire?"

"I think I need to do Ho'o'ponopono with Pele."

"Pele? The volcano goddess?"

"Yes. Years ago, I hiked to the edge of the crater. I mean *right* to the edge. I was right next to the camera that they have perched on the precipice to monitor the volcanic activity."

"You went right up to the edge?"

"Yes."

"And you're still alive…"

"Yes."

"Pele could have killed you in a second. She must have been okay with it. You don't need to do Ho'o'ponopono with her. There's nothing to ask forgiveness for."

I went back to my seat, the reality of how much danger I had put myself in truly sinking in for the first time. I silently sent gratitude to Pele for sparing my life.

And today, as I sat in my bed, trying to fall asleep, I felt I was ready to do Ho'oponopono with my mom. To ask for her forgiveness. I took a few deep breaths, called an image of her to mind, and began to say, "I forgive you. Do you forgive me too?" over and over.

Instead of staying on stage like she's 'supposed to,' the image of my mom came right up to me, cupped my face in her hands, and said, "You're fine, Boo. There's nothing to forgive." Then she kissed me on my forehead like I kiss my son each day, and calmly walked away.

37
Pathway to God

As I approached my favorite spot on the rocky beach, I saw a young man, sitting in the sun.

"Beautiful day," I said.

"Yes it is. Are you swimming to Ka'awaloa?"

I had a neoprene diving hat on and had my snorkel perched atop my head, but my puzzled look was nevertheless distinguishable.

"The monument. Are you swimming to the monument?"

"Oh, yes. That's my daily ocean therapy. What did you call it?"

"Ka'awaloa. That's the traditional Hawaiian name for the cove on the other side of the bay."

At this point, I knew I had to ask a question that had been circling in my mind for weeks…

"Can I ask you a strange question?"

"Sure."

"My mom died in this bay. I was wondering if there is any lore or Hawaiian historical significance to that."

"Well, this bay has always been sacred to the Hawaiian people. Only the royalty — the alii — were allowed here on the beach where we are now.

And ley lines cross here.

But I'd say the most significant thing about this bay is the name — Kealakekua — which means Pathway to the gods. And the original name was Kea la ke akua, which means Pathway to God."

Full body chills.

"Your mom is with you every day. In the water, the fish… She's in everything now. The trick is to learn that while we're alive — that we are already one with everything. Death isn't the end. She's with you."

"After she died, I read that according to Greek mythology, dolphins carry souls from this world to the next. We were swimming with the dolphins here when she died, so I can hope that she went from bliss to…"

"Bliss. Bliss to bliss."

"Yes." I smiled. "I'm so glad I met you."

And then we embraced.

38
Dreamtime

That night I had a dream about the scene that used to loop in my head during the most intense moments of my grief — the scene where I walk into the hospital room and find my mother lying lifeless on the table.

But this wasn't a loop, replaying in my brain. It was a dream. So the rules had changed.

I didn't scream. Or cry. Or try to escape the reality of that moment. I simply walked up to my mom and gently placed my hands on her body.

Her toes began to wiggle, she opened her eyes, and she sat up.

She looked at me with eyes only a mother has for her child, and she said, "I'm OK, Boo. You can let go." And then she got up off the table and left.

Huna tells us that our Higher Self speaks to us in dreams, bringing us wisdom that our conscious mind would not otherwise have access to.

The dreamworld, so the shamans say, is just as real as the physical world. In fact, many indigenous populations across the globe believe that the physical world is dreamed into existence, and that our nighttime dreams are closer to the source of reality than our waking moments.

Sometimes our dreams are cryptic, so there is a shamanic practice of dream interpretation that helps us decipher the messages that arrive during our adventures in the dreamworld.

This one didn't need any interpretation.

It only required me to listen.

39
Aumakua

'Aumakua' is the Huna term for Higher Self—the part of you that is all-knowing, ever-present, and is connected to the Great Spirit. 'Aumakua' is also the name given to guardian or ancestral spirits. According to Hawaiian lore, when family members pass away, they become aumakua, watching over the living from the Spirit world.

Aumakua can take the form of animals, plants, rocks, or sometimes all three, to guide and protect family members here on the Earthly plane.

You'll recognize your aumakua in nature, say the shamans, by the sensation you feel in your belly. Just like your Higher Self, your ancestors speak to you through your na'au.

You can honor your aumakua by respecting the animal itself, and by listening to the messages that come to you while in its presence. When you do this, your connection with your ancestors deepens, your connection to your na'au deepens, and you open the channels to be guided from the Spirit world.

40
Manta

I was on my way back across the bay, just about a quarter mile from shore, when a gorgeous manta ray swam beneath me. She was between 6 and 7 feet from wingtip to wingtip, gliding gracefully just above the ocean floor.

"Hi Mom," I said in my mind.

I stayed with the manta, giving her space, sending love and aloha as I watched from about 30 feet away.

Then she came quite close—just a few feet below me.

I remembered that day with my mom. Before swimming off to play with the dolphins, I had swum beneath her— 'mermaiding' as I call it—looking up at her, my belly facing hers, smiling and waving as if I were a sea creature making interspecies contact.

I thought about doing that with the manta—diving beneath her, doing my mermaid impression—but I hesitated for just a second because I didn't want to frighten her.

In that second of hesitation, the manta began to twist. She turned over, showing me *her* belly, and floating up to just about a foot beneath me.

We swam that way for about 10 minutes, each of us with our most vulnerable surface facing the other, in total trust.

In Hawaiian culture, the name of the manta — hahalua — can be interpreted as 'two breaths.' 'Ha,' meaning 'breath,' and 'lua,' meaning 'two.' Occasionally the mantas will breach, and legend says that when they jump out of the water, they bring their experience from below into our world, offering us their wisdom from the other side.

This one didn't have to jump. Her ultimate display of faith in me as a kind being, worthy of her soft underbelly, was more than enough.

41
Make More Peace

I was sitting on the beach after my swim, thawing. Yes, even in Hawaii, I get cold after an hour in the water. I have become totally Soft.

My thoughts inevitably wandered to that fateful day when I lost my mom. I used to imagine her last moments full of struggle and fear. But today was different.

Today I saw her swimming with the dolphins. Giggling. Just like I *actually* saw her doing that day. I saw her resting on the top of the water, effortlessly, as you can do with fins and a snorkel, mesmerized by the beauty of the dolphins.

I saw her smile. The corners of her mouth upturned even with the snorkel mouthpiece obstructing a full smile. And her eyes crinkled in the way they do only when a smile is genuine.

And then she went still.

All of a sudden, she just *stopped*.

I got the chills.

And I whispered out to the ocean, as my throat closed with the swelling sadness inside of me, "Were you happy?"

More chills.

"So it was OK?"

Then I heard, "Thank you, Claire. Thank you."

"What now?" I asked.

"Carry on. Make more peace."

Thirteen years ago, when my mom took me through the future-self visualization for the first time, I asked my older, wiser self for some sage advice.

"Make peace with your family," she said.

I thought that meant forgiving my grandmother for the way she treated my dad as a child.

Ten years ago, I flew to Philadelphia when Grandma's caregiver at the nursing facility called to say she had taken a turn for the worse. "She'll make it through this," he had said, "but she doesn't have long. You might want to come now, while she's lucid."

So my mom and I went. I went because I knew my mom was more tapped into what the right thing to do was, and I hadn't seen my grandma in a few years.

Mom and I went the day after we got the call. We arrived in Philly at 2 a.m., went to the car rental place, and while we were being checked in, we got a call from Medford Leas.

My grandmother had just died.

We missed her by an hour.

We drove straight to the facility, and I went in to sit with her.

I talked with her. I kissed her. I held her hand. She was still warm, and it was as if she was still in the room with me. Maybe she was.

I saw her shoes in the corner, and I could see her standing in them. They were resting at the edge of the room in just the way they used to sit on her feet. Both toes pointing in just the slightest bit. The right heel askew a bit more than the left. And the shoes were the same shoes as always—comfortable, practical shoes designed to look like high-class flats. She used to wear them gardening years before. Because, you know, we must always look good.

I cried. Soft, slow tears. Not like the violent ones I'd cry for my mom a decade later.

I forgave her for all the things she had done that I perceived as wrong, and I asked her for forgiveness for all the ways I thought I had fallen short as a grandchild.

I thought *that* was the peace that I had been instructed to make. The peace with my grandma.

Now, of course, I realized making peace with my mom was just as critical. And I was getting the same message again — Make more peace.

I guess I'm not done.

Maybe we never are.

42
Pō

Pō is the Hawaiian word for 'night,' 'darkness,' and 'the ancient realm from which life originated.' Pō is both our beginning and our end, say the Hawaiians, since it is from Pō that we emerge when our spirits are born into physical bodies, and back to Pō that we return when our time here on Earth is complete. Pō is pure nothingness, while also being the source of ultimate possibilities.

Pō is a realm that the shamans can visit on purpose, to perform healings. One such technique that takes you into the Pō is called the Keawe Process, and its purpose is to help you reconcile an inner conflict.

This inner battle could be between two warring thoughts, beliefs, paths to take in life, or even yourself and an addiction. The Keawe Process un-creates the tension, the fight, the conflict, and the result is complete alignment. Sometimes one side of the conflict disappears, leaving just one answer, and sometimes a third, previously unknown option appears. In all cases, what's left after the healing is a singular path that's in line with who you are at your core.

As the brave souls who are gay and transgender have taught us, we are who we are. Not even the physical bodies we are born with can dictate who we are or who we should become. There is an inner knowing, a compass, a true North within each of us, and nothing can alter that. Not society. Not church. Not our parents. Not the government. Not our own self-judgments. Nothing.

The Keawe Process connects you to that inner compass that already knows your answers.

So today, after my swim, I decided I was ready to end the inner conflict that had plagued me for as long as I could remember. I was ready to surrender to the truth of who I am. To do the Keawe Process on *the biggie* – Who I Am and Who I Think I Should Be.

My journey thus far had told me that's the key. Love who you are. Don't resist it. Don't try to become who you think you're *supposed* to be. It's painful. And futile.

I had been asked to surrender. To surrender to truth – whether that was pain in my heart, a pull from the Earth that told me where I belonged, a message to let go of the guilt surrounding my mom's death, or a connection to who I really am.

I was ready for complete surrender.

The Keawe Process is a visualization, and part of it entails dropping in and 'becoming' one of the conflicting parts. You do this while looking across a beam of light at the other part. So I decided to embody Who I Am, and to look across the beam of light at Who I Should Be.

But there was nothing there. Nothing except a few molecules attempting to organize themselves into a wispy image. And after a few short moments, even those disappeared.

There was no part of me that felt I should be different than who I am.

No more conflict.

No more war.

Pono.

43
Chocolate

My scalp began to tingle, and my internal temperature rose. The feeling slowly trickled down my face and neck, as if someone were pouring a pitcher of warm, effervescent honey on my head. The sensation traveled to my shoulders, down my arms, and into my hands. My fingertips became alive with a gentle electricity.

"Mom?" I said aloud.

I heard, "Now you have *my* talents too."

Those gifted with the ability to communicate with Spirit have told me that grief inhibits one's ability to receive messages from the other side. Grief, they say, has such a dissonant frequency. All you hear is static, even when your loved ones are broadcasting in your direction.

I guess I had walked, climbed, and swum my way to a place where my internal radio could get the full transmission now.

Of course, those same gifted individuals also say never to allow a 'foreign energy' to enter your body. But I never did follow rules. And my heart said this one was okay.

After the honey had filled my entire upper body, I looked down at my right arm. "I have my mother's hands," I said to myself. Covered in freckles, veins popping out.

"Thank you for these hands," I said as I kissed one of the brown spots on the back of my right hand near my wrist.

I felt a little hungry.

"Soma, do we have any chocolate?"

"Chocolate? You want chocolate? Are you okay?"

Nobody has ever mistakenly labeled me 'normal,' but not having a special place in my heart for chocolate might be one of my most frequently questioned qualities. My mother, of course, was a chocolate fiend.

I don't have anything *against* chocolate, so sometimes I would partake in her ceremonious consumption of truffles. She'd bring three pristine chocolate delights out on a small plate of fine china, and we would take turns taking the teensiest bites out of each one.

"Assume the truffle pose," she'd say with a giggle, and we'd both pucker our lips and stick our front teeth out, like we were mimicking beavers or rabbits. Then she'd take the absolute smallest bite of a truffle, and pass it to me so I could do the same. We would repeat this ritual, taking rabbit nibbles of truffle number one, then number two, then number three, and back to number one, until we'd consumed every morsel.

But I never ate chocolate alone, unceremoniously, without assuming the truffle pose.

Until now.

I *had* to find some chocolate. *Not* eating chocolate was not an option in this moment.

"Yeah, chocolate," I called out to my husband. "iGan must be craving it on the other side."

"I think we have some chocolate chips in the fridge."

"That'll do!"

I stuck my hand in the bag, grabbed more chips than I'd probably eaten in my entire life, raised my fist of chocolate up to the heavens, and said, "Here's to you, Maw!"

44
Dance

I was just a few minutes from shore. The water was cloudy, as was the sky, so it was a bit like swimming in pale blue milk.

Through the near-opaque water, I saw something dark. It began to rise in the water, spiraling up towards me.

A manta ray.

The manta ray.

My friend, the manta ray who has my mother's eyes.

In this moment, she also had my mother's propensity to dance at the slightest provocation. Wings outstretched, gracefully flying through the water, she came to my left side, her right wingtip mere inches from my face.

I giggled.

Trying not to move a muscle in hopes that she'd come close again, I caught the manta's eye, and sensed that she was a bit bored with my response to her ballet.

Slowly, I uncurled my 'wings,' dove down, and did my hillbilly best at flying through the water like my aquatic friend. She was intrigued, it seemed, as she ramped up her own display, somersaulting backwards while moving towards me, so we met belly-to-belly for a moment.

I dove again, did a barrel roll, and came out flapping my wings. She responded by taking another few elegant passes through the water, swimming in a large circle around me.

Then she dove deep, taking her dance where I could not follow.

"Thanks for the visit, Mom," I said quietly as I put my hands first to my chest, and then out towards the manta, sending her my love, and a promise that I'd be back tomorrow.

My dance partner.
~photo by Lisa Denning

45
Happy Birthingday

Today is my birthday. My first birthday without Mom.

She would have called it my *birthingday.*

I tossed and turned all last night. I wasn't UP like that fateful night of October 11. I was just restless. Anxious. My heart was beating far faster than it needed to for sleep, and it kept me from relaxing fully, even when I did doze off.

I woke up every few hours and peed, but I do think I cobbled together a good 5 or so hours of shut-eye. That's more than many get on a good night, I realize. So no complaints.

When my alarm went off at 6:17 I felt OK. Not exhausted. Not too irritable, but profoundly *sad.*

I'm not at war with myself anymore. And I'm not at war with the memory of my mother. She's with me now, riding sidecar to my brain and heart, offering ideas, words, and hugs from across the veil.

My anger, guilt, and shame have dissipated.

But my sadness remains.

I'm only now becoming acquainted with sadness as an emotion to be embraced. Not feared. Or hidden. Or looked down upon as a sign of weakness.

There is something almost comforting about sadness. Something *pure.*

Sadness reminds me of the good times. The silly times. The heartfelt times. The moments I replay over and over in my mind because they make me *smile.*

Sadness is perhaps the tail-end of grief, but I have the sense that it's an eternal tail. One that stays with you as a constant reminder of love.

I've found that this tail of sadness, like a cat's physical tail, keeps me balanced. It keeps me present. Reminds me of the fullness of life. Of what's important. And, possibly more helpful, what's *not* important. This tail reminds me to look into the eyes of those who remain with me, and to feel the love that's so sweet, it too, has a twinge of sadness in it.

Today is a sad day, but that doesn't make it a *bad* day.

I'm simply acutely aware of the missing player on this anniversary of my appearance onto the Earthly stage.

No one is going to call me today and sing *Happy Birthday*, and then proceed to tell me the story of my birth — How much pain I put my mother through. How the doctors yanked me out with forceps, giving me two huge bruises on the sides of my head for weeks. How when I finally emerged, and my mother was being stitched up from the enormous episiotomy, that I wouldn't breathe. How I was starting to turn blue, and the doctor leaned in to give me mouth-to-mouth, and my father fainted in the delivery room, which prompted the doctor who was bent over my tiny body to say, "Get him out of here!" No stories of how I grabbed the doctor's thumb with my little hand once I began to breathe, reassuring everyone that although I wasn't good at following orders, falling in line, or making it easy for others, at least I was strong.

No "Tell me everything, Boo" today.

No "What would make this year magical?"

No "Sooo…. When are you coming to visit your ole maw?"

No package of cookies I can't eat (she was on board with no flour, but couldn't fathom someone could react to *sugar*, so she kept sending well-intentioned confectionary delights that I had to give away.) No purple and turquoise 'doodads' as she called them—socks, little pouches, journals, pens, all the unnecessary but fun and frivolous things she always sent. No card with *Claire-Dee-Boo* in perfect calligraphy on the front.

None of that is coming today.

None of that is ever coming. Today is the first of all future birthdays that will be celebrated without the woman who birthed me.

The sadness is *large*, as my mom would say, so I do what I always do to feel better.

I go to the ocean.

The dolphins have been at my swimming hole for about 10 days in a row, so I'm feeling especially relaxed and open to whatever is in store for me. I know I'm going to get the silky turquoise and azure water, and that's enough.

I park my car and get my gear ready, and as I'm walking out to my favorite spot on the rocky shore, I see fins. Feeling extremely blessed, I get ready, and walk into the water. There aren't any waves to speak of, and the water is warm.

So far so good.

For some reason, the dolphins tend to move further away from shore the moment I get in. Sometimes I wonder if it's because they know I want my exercise. Or maybe it's their way of winking at me, telling me to follow them out further than the tourists will go, so we can have the ocean to ourselves.

Or maybe it's just coincidence. They are, after all, *dolphins*, and I'm sure they have more important things to do than orchestrate their entire swimming routine around little ole me.

Whatever the reason, they do the same thing today. With one or two flicks of their tails, they scoot out another half mile.

No worries. I'm fully satisfied with the turquoise water. But I haven't gone completely mad or docile in my posttraumatic peace. Dolphins are still the pinnacle of coolness and wisdom in my book, so I keep swimming.

And there they are.

Twenty gorgeous spinner dolphins, right there, on *my* birthday. I think, "Maybe I *will* take a moment to celebrate!"

They swim past me, and I'm about to follow, when another thirty appear behind me. And then to my right, in come another fifty.

One hundred dolphins coming from all sides. Swimming, twirling, squeaking.

This is my kind of birthday party!

One comes up to me, looks me in the eye, and blows some bubbles from her blowhole.

I look back at her, and blow bubbles in return.

She blows some more.

And back and forth we go until (I imagine) she grows tired of swimming so slowly, and she swims ahead, blowing a trail of bubbles that I swim through for the next several minutes, giggling as I hear the cute 'pop' sound as each bubble bursts on my skin.

Not to be outdone, a young male who I'd played with several times recently comes over to me and gives me the 'howzit' head-bob.

I return the gesture.

He waves his flippers back and forth.

I wave my 'flippers' too.

He's quite close to me, on my left side, so I'm swimming sideways through the water. Since I don't have eyes on the sides of my head like he does, I'm doing my best to give him my full attention without straining my neck.

So, in our game of mimicry that I have deemed the 'I love you' game, because we mimic those we admire, and it's what I feel when I do it, and, why not?, this cute teenage dolphin comes up to the surface of the water and turns himself sideways, modeling what I'm doing with my body. He puts his back to me, perhaps to reassure me that he's not looking for sex as so many of them are, and then he rights himself to his normal orientation and resumes the head-bob and flipper-flap motions of our 'I love you' game.

Seeing that there's clearly something special happening here, the entire pod decides to come over.

There we are. Me in all my gear, in awe of the dolphins, and my finned friend, possibly curious or amused by me, and every last pod member comes by.

One by one, two by two, and sometimes ten by ten, they swim to my right side, many coming just inches from

170

me. Some look at me with their open eye, and others keep their open eye on their pod and say hello with their sonar.

But they all come by.

I feel so seen. So held. So nurtured. And so accepted.

Maybe they knew I needed a little extra mothering today.

And maybe, just maybe, if I sink into this feeling of being seen, held, nurtured, and accepted by Nature, I can sink into the arms of the Cosmic Mother when I need her, no matter where I am, or whether any of my finned friends are present.

Thank you, Mom.

It's because of you that I've arrived here.

You always told me to hold others as whole, resourceful, and creative beings.

I'm sure you looked down at me 42 years ago and saw me as whole, resourceful, and creative.

What a miracle you'd just given birth to.

We lost our way for a while there, but we've both found it again, I believe.

I am whole, and I finally see myself as such.

And you. You are the ocean. The trees. The fish. The dolphins. The manta rays. You are everything. A miracle I get to behold every day.

Thank you.

Acknowledgments

More creatures than I have space to name here came together to make this book possible. To my mother, I thank you for your life, my life, and the incredible lessons I learned from your death. To the spinner dolphins, my gratitude for your magic, your healing, and your ability to connect me to my deepest Self. To Soma, for your unending devotion and belief in me. To Felix, for a love so pure that it penetrated even my deepest moments of grief. To my dad, for both understanding the depth of my pain, and for helping to keep my mother's memory alive with levity by building the list of Betty-isms. Her silliness is sure to live on forever now. To Danielle, for crying with me on the phone, laughing with me on the beach, and for being my biggest fan. To Rysa, for knowing I had this story in me. To my friends and family near and wide, whom I regularly neglected during my interminable bouts of solitude and swimming, thank you for seeing me, and knowing I do love you. To Lisa, for your connection with the sea creatures and your photographic genius, continually combining to produce the most magical images. To Ewan, my editor and dear friend across the globe, your encouragement, honesty, and generosity pulled me through the eye of this needle, and have already propelled me forward on to my next act of creation.

To you, dear reader, thank you for accompanying me on this journey. May my words bring you a little closer to your heart. To your path. May they guide you home.

All my love,
Claire

APPENDIX 1:
Nai'a Healing Questionnaire

This questionnaire is meant to spark a conversation between your everyday conscious self and your deeper, possibly hidden, Self. This is an inquiry, not a graded quiz or a to-do list. It is designed to get you thinking.

Many people find it useful to use a scale from 1-10 in responding to the statements in Part 1. You can also simply say 'yes' or 'no.' Whatever you do, I ask that you honor the answer you receive. Acknowledge it. Recognize that, for example, you may not feel comfortable expressing your uniqueness. With that awareness, you can continue to gently ask more questions. Why? What would need to be different for you to feel comfortable? Is there a piece of you that you have not yet given a voice? Can you let that part speak now?

Be both compassionate and brutally honest with yourself. And let whatever answer you get be okay. Your inner wisdom will begin to chew on this in the background of your life. If you become hungry for more, contact me at Claire@ClaireElisabeth.com and I'll help you find your next step.

Part 1

1 - I get insights, epiphanies, downloads, and/or gut feelings.

2 - I act on these insights.

3 - I have moments of being in Flow, or in the Zone.

4 - I know what my top values are. (Ex: freedom, dignity, clarity, fun)

5 - My life allows for me to live my top values.

6 - I allow myself to feel my emotions fully (vs judging them and stuffing them.)

7 - I feel safe to pursue my heart's desires.

8 - I have a practice/activity that quiets the voice in my head. (Yes, we all have that voice.)

10 - I feel comfortable in my own skin.

15 - I express myself and my uniqueness fully.

11 - I allow others to see me for who I am.

12 - I can be myself at home.

13 - I can be myself at work.

14 - I can be myself with my friends.

15 - I am living a life that is true to who I am.

Part 2 is designed to get you thinking a bit deeper, and will likely require at least a sentence or two to answer each question. The more open and honest you are with your answers, the more potential there is for healing. And remember, while being your true, fully expressed Self may be loud and flamboyant, or quiet and contained, your true Self always acts from love.

Part 2

1 - If you were to be yourself without apology, what, if anything, about your behavior would change?

2 - Do you feel like you sometimes give up who you are in order to please others? When? With whom? What do you hope to gain? What do you lose in the process?

3 - If you didn't give one rat's patootie about others' judgments of you, would you live your life differently? How?

APPENDIX 2:
GLOSSARY OF
HAWAIIAN TERMS

Aumakua — The Huna term for Higher Self. Also, the ancestral spirits who guide and protect family members. Aumakua can take the form of animals, plants, or rocks in order to help those living on the Earthly plane.

Ho'oponopono — A Hawaiian forgiveness process. This used to be an in-person process, but is now practiced as an energetic healing technique.

Huna — The ancient Hawaiian art and science of healing and spiritual development. The word 'huna' means 'secret.' The healing practice of Huna bears that name because for many years the teachings were kept secret.

Keawe process — An energetic healing process where tension and stress are un-created. The Keawe process heals conflicts between people as well as inner conflict within oneself.

Na'au — The belly, and the seat of intuition according to Hawaiian wisdom. Your Higher Self speaks to you via your na'au, so gut feelings are considered sacred.

Nai'a — The Hawaiian name for 'dolphin.' Also used to describe free-spirited people who follow their hearts.

Pō — The Hawaiian word for 'night,' 'darkness,' and 'the ancient realm from which life originated.' It is pure nothingness, while also being the source of ultimate possibilities. The Keawe Process takes you into the Pō to perform healings.

Pono — Fully aligned with yourself. When you are pono, you are internally congruent and right with yourself.

APPENDIX 3:
GLOSSARY OF BETTY-ISMS

Words always had a special place in my mom's heart. To her, they weren't just tools, already forged, to be used in the construction of sentences. No, for her, words were malleable, soft, allowing. Beckoning to be altered.

Words morphed in my mother's presence.

Here is an undoubtedly incomplete list of the words that made their way into my language from hers:

Ackleast — at least

Ackventure — adventure

Birthingday — birthday

Bunloon — balloon

Cacaloo — calculator

Confabulations — congratulations

Couch radishes — couch potatoes

Degredients — ingredients

Deloris — delirious

Disirregardlessly — regardless

Eblow — elbow

Fangers — fingers

Fragrant — pregnant

Furhats — perhaps

Gangrene hour — cranky time of day (originated when I was a little kid, but it applies to people of all ages)

Gaposis — gap (anything from the space between Billy's teeth to the years between marriages)

Gorjesus — gorgeous

Gradoo — sticky icky stuff

Hee-keem — ice cream

Horsey-doovers — hor d'oeuvres

Ly-tion-ful-ness — a string of suffixes added to any word for emphasis

Mecidine (pronounced messidin) — medicine

Nakrim — napkin

Ossmo — almost

Perhunks — perhaps

Removilate — remove

Sliverduties — silverware

Snackerel (rhymes with mackerel) — snack

Sweatpants — used in place of any noun that can't be remembered. Ex: I went to the Botanic Gardens yesterday and the...uh...*sweatpants* were in full bloom.

Tabable — table

Thraboom — bathroom

Toidy-poopers — toilet paper

Van Nuys — very nice

Xaustiflated (pronounced zaustiflated) — exhausted

APPENDIX 4:
GUIDELINES FOR SWIMMING WITH DOLPHINS

These guidelines for swimming with aloha are reproduced with permission from the Hawaii Dolphin Initiative, a non-profit organization in service of fostering beneficial relationships between humans and dolphins.

Thank you for following these guidelines, for helping us keep this healing avenue open and safe, and for respecting our wise and generous cetacean friends.

1- Allow nai'a to *choose* when, if, and how they would like to interact with you. If you come across dolphins while swimming, allow them to approach you if they so choose. If you stay calm, curious dolphins may swim around you or swim alongside you. *Stop and float, or swim very slowly.*

2- Respect quiet, slow moving dolphins. They may be resting. Dolphins sometimes swim slowly in groups (pods), with one eye open and one eye closed. They are likely *resting.* If you are swimming close to quiet, slow moving dolphins, follow their example. *Move slowly or simply float around resting dolphins. Do NOT disturb!*

3- Swim with your arms by your side. Overhand swimming can be disruptive to the nai'a. They may then move away from you. If you swim without fins, slow breaststroke is best. *Avoid splashing the water if dolphins are around.*

4- Do not pursue, touch, or feed the nai'a. Please do not aggressively swim toward, attempt to dive on top of, or intercept the dolphins, as this may cause them unnecessary stress. *Touching or feeding nai'a may be harmful to their health.*

5- Show respect and aloha to your fellow swimmers. Dolphins are sensitive beings. They appreciate respectful behavior in the water. Even if you can swim faster than someone else, wait your turn. Do not interfere with a special moment another swimmer may be experiencing. *Do NOT harass the dolphins or your fellow swimmers.*

RESOURCES

Spirit Is Calling — Owned and operated by Carmen Figueras, the woman who introduced me to both meditation and dolphins. Her non-profit organization teaches meditation classes, runs clairvoyant training programs, and takes pilgrims all over the world on spiritual adventures.
SpiritIsCalling.com

Bowl of Light — **a book by Hank Wesselman**
From the Amazon description:
In 1996, a revered Hawaiian elder befriended an American anthropologist, and from their rare and intimate rapport, something miraculous emerged. Through the words and teachings of the *kahuna* wisdom-keeper Hale Makua, Dr. Hank Wesselman was gifted with an enhanced perspective into the sacred knowledge of ancient Hawaii.
SharedWisdom.com

Hawaii Dolphin Initiative — A non-profit organization on the Big Island of Hawaii that trains volunteers to educate the public on respectful dolphin interaction. Their goal is to keep swimming with wild spinner dolphins legal by teaching people how to properly be with the dolphins in the water.
HawaiiDolphinInitiative.org

Huna Higher Consciousness Trainings — Dr. Matt James offers training in the ancient Hawaiian art of Huna. All of his trainings follow the Bray family lineage. Huna.com

Ocean Eyes Photography — Lisa Denning is the photographer extraordinaire who took all the photos in this book, minus the three of me. She has a spirit as dear and magical as the dolphins themselves, and spends much of her life connecting with aquatic creatures across the globe.
LisaDenning.com

ABOUT THE AUTHOR

Claire Elisabeth is a writer, teacher, and some would say, dolphin whisperer. She has the uncanny ability to see the truth of who you are, and to help you see it too. Claire has spent her life looking into people's hearts and helping them find the power in who they already are. She lives on the Big Island of Hawaii with her husband, son, cat, and father, and spends as much time as she can in the ocean with her non-human relatives, the spinner dolphins. *Reconcile* is her first book. You can learn more about Claire and her work at ClaireElisabeth.com.

65592627R00110

Made in the USA
Middletown, DE
08 September 2019